AF553368

WORKERS' PARTICIPATION IN MANAGEMENT

Ch. S. Durga Prasad

DISCOVERY PUBLISHING HOUSE
NEW DELHI (INDIA)—110 002

First Published 1995

Reprinted-2011

ISBN 81-7141-271-8

Published by :

DISCOVERY PUBLISHING HOUSE
4831/24, Ansari Road, Prahlad Street,
Darya Ganj, New Delhi-110002 (India)
Phone: 23279245 • Fax: 91-11-23253475
E-mail:dphtemp@indiatimes.com

Laser Typesetting by :

Allied Computers,
Karnal

Printed at:
Mehra Offset Press
Delhi

Dedicated to

My Beloved

GRANDPARENTS

Late Sri Kalagara Venkata Ratnam Chowdery,
and
Late Smt. Kalagara Sakuntala Devi.

Preface

The role of human resources is more vital than any other resources in the conversion process of input into output. In fact, the entire industrialization depends on effective utilization of human resources and maintenance of sound industrial relations. Industrial relations situation in India was disturbed by frequent industrial disputes. Further, the Government and employers could not get the unreserved co-operation of employees. Workers extend unreserved co-operation only when they are socially and psychologically involved in the entire process of management. Workers' participation in management develops mutual trust, commitment of the employees and improves industrial harmony.

The Works Committees—a scheme of workers' participation in management—constituted under the Industrial Disputes Act of 1947 were required to meet every month and discuss issues relating to production, absenteeism, discipline, safety, health, welfare and working conditions. The Works Committees failed to cope with the needs of the industry and workers. The Government introduced Joint Management Councils (JMCs) a scheme of participative management in 1956. The function of the JMCs as decided by the Indian Labour Conference in the year 1957 are (a) information sharing (b) consultation and (c) administration of standing orders, introduction of changes in methods and techniques of production and to discuss matters such as safety, welfare and training programmes.

Another form of participative management in the Indian context has been to give opportunities to workers to represent their view points through nomination of their representatives on the board of directors in some public sector units in the year 1971. Later it was also introduced in the nationalized banks in 1973.

The next important step in experimenting workers' participation was the Governments' recommendation in October 1975 to set up shop councils at the shop or departmental level and joint councils at the enterprise level in those undertakings which have employment of 500 or more workers in the manufacturing and units of public, private and co-operative sectors. The major functions of shop councils are, to improve productivity, reduction of absenteeism, maintain general discipline, maintain congenial working conditions, establish two-way communication etc. The joint council's functions are efficiency and fixation of productivity, norms of man and the machine as a whole, to deal the matters which remain unresolved at the shop council, maintenance of congenial working conditions etc.

In 1983 the Government extended the scheme by introducing apex level councils.

India adopted the mixed economic system in pursuit of the socialistic pattern of society. The public sector plays most crucial role by instituting core industry like steel, heavy electricals, electronics etc., whereas the private sector concentrates on other industries. Among the public sector units BHEL is one of the successful organizations. It ranks among the top 500 companies in the world and occupies sixth rank among the public sector organizations in India. The Tata Iron and Steel Company Limited occupies first place among the private sector organizations in respect of turnover in India. Maintenance of congenial industrial Relations is the vital feature of both the organizations. These two organizations were selected for the study, in view of this background.

BHEL introduced the scheme of participative management in the form of Bi-partite joint committee at apex level in the year 1973. It extended the scope of joint committees to grass-root and plant level with the names of shop councils and joint councils in the year 1975. In TISCO, the first joint committee was constituted in 1919 much before the introduction of the schemes by the Government. It was revived again in 1946 by establishing the different councils for various zones. The present scheme of closer association of employees with the management has been in operation since 1956 with three-tier structure i.e., Joint Departmental Council at grass-root level, Joint Works Council at plant level and Joint Consultative Council of Management at apex level.

There are altogether 15 councils in BHEL and 49 councils in TISCO with equal representation of management and workers. The important objectives of participative management councils in both the organizations are to (a) increase production, (b) provision of better health, safety measures and (c) satisfy the urge for self-expression.

The imperfect functioning of involuntary participation gave birth to a new concept called quality circles. This scheme is a voluntary association of workers to discuss work related problems and offer suggestions to management. This scheme is expected to play complimentary role to workers' participation in management. BHEL introduced the quality circles first time in India in the year 1981. The number of quality circles in BHEL, Ramachandrapuram unit increased to 352 in 1988-89. TISCO introduced quality circles in 1986 and the number increased to 12 in 1988-89.

The present study has been carried out with the help of and assistance extended by several people at various stages. I take this opportunity to express my thanks to them.

It is my pleasure and privilege to acknowledge and express my deep sense of gratitude to my teacher and Research Director, Professor P. Subba Rao, Sri Krishnadevaraya Institute of Management, Sri Krishanadevaraya University, Anantpur who inspired and initiated me to make this study. Despite his busy academic and administrative schedule, he has always been kind enough to spare his valuable time and thought in giving necessary guidance. Barring his involvement and inspiration the study is not imaginable.

I express my sincere thanks to Professor S. Subbaramaiah, Dean of Management, Prof. L. Venugopal Reddy, Head of the Department, Dr. Ch. Rama Prasada Rao, and Dr. Muthyalu Naidu of Sri Krishnadevaraya Institute of Management, S. K. University for their encouragement.

Sincere thanks are due to the authorities of S.K. University for providing facilities to carry out the work.

I am also grateful to Professor M. Gangadhara Rao garu, Faculty of Commerce and Management Studies, Andhra University, Waltair for his continuous encouragement throughout my career and offering suggestions at every stage of this project.

I am specially thankful to Sri K. Sudhakar, Director P.G. Courses, Sri V. Krishnaji Rao former Principal and Sri M.S.V. Sarma, Principal, Sir C.R.R. College for the encouragement they have given me during my research.

I express my gratefulness to Prof. B.S. Murthy, Department of Human Resources Management, Dr. M. Madhusudhana Rao, Prof. C. Suryanarayana, Prof. D. Panduranga Rao, Head, Department of Commerce and Management Studies, Andhra University, Sri. K. Nageswara Rao and Sri Ramanujam of Sir C.R.R. College, Eluru for their generous encouragement and affection.

I am particularly grateful to Sri N.S. Tallur, Deputy General Manager, Human Resources Development Centre, Sri N.N. Singh, Deputy General Manager (Personnel), Sri R.S.R.V. Krishna Rao, Senior Personnel Officer, Sri B. Subramanian, Manager, Quality Assurance Division, Sri N. Nagarajan, Senior Manager, HRDC of Bharat Heavy Electricals Limited, Ramachandrapuram, Hyderabad, Sri K.P. Varma, Director (Personnel), Sri V.M. Sinha, Chief Industrial Relations Manager, Joint Consultations, Sri Jaideo Upadhyaya, Sri Vasudevan, Mrs. Radha, Sri C.S. Pandey of The Tata Iron and Steel Company Limited, Jamshedpur and Sri S.R. Udpa, Executive Director, Quality Circle Forum of India, Hyderabad and the members of participative councils and quality circles who helped me during data collection.

My sincere thanks are due to all my friends, co-research scholars and my family members who helped me at various stages of this work.

Words are insufficient to express my profound sense of gratitude to my grandfather late Sri Kalagara Venkata Ratnam whose encouragement and blessings gave me a great physical and moral strength throughout my career as well as in the present investigation.

I am grateful to Mrs. P. Rama Devi for her affection towards me during my stay in Anantapur.

I am also thankful to Sri N. Hemakshi Achari, Sri K.K. Azam Khan and Sri P. Lokanna for neat execution of typing.

However, I alone assume the complete responsibility for any errors that might have crept in or omissions that are committed unconsciously.

Ch. S. Durga Prasad

Contents

Contents

Introduction

Industrial Relations : An Overview

1. Need for Harmonious Relations

Industrial Relations is that part of management which is concerned with the manpower of the enterprise[1]. The importance of establishing and maintaining harmonious relations between employers and employees needs no emphasis. Mere technical efficiency, up-to-date machinery, good plant lay-out and dynamic Organization are not enough to make a business profitable; good human relations in industry plays almost a decisive role in this respect. The fundamental purpose of industrial relations is to increase industrial production by securing harmonious relationship among labour, management, and capital thereby promoting the economic prosperity of a nation. The term `industrial harmony, refers to harmony between persons or groups of persons- particularly labour and management, the two major partners of industrial community[2]. Industrial harmony necessitates the creation of an industrial order in which the two major partners accept the actual situation as such, and willingly work together inspite of their differences at opinions. This requires the development of mutual confidence in the abilities and intentions of the parties. Confidence is a form of capital i.e., just as much a pre-requisite

1. Bethel, L.L., Atwater, F.J., Smith, G.H.E., and Steackman, H.A., "*Industrial Organization and Management*", McGraw-Hill Book Company Inc., New York, 1971, p. 385.
2. Gupta, Manju "*Industrial Relations in Ship Building Industry*," Andhra University Press, Waltair, 1978, p.1.

for industrial change as any other form. If either party proposes a change in a technical and social organization of a plant, that change will go into effect only if the other party has enough confidence in the first to wait and see the results of the change and suspend judgement. "Confidence is a form of capital that must be spent to get change, and if the change is accepted by the parties favourable, the capital is restored."[1] If the objective is to have expanding, flexible, social fields, this confidence is absolutely essential.

Further, industrial harmony involves "the conditions of substantial justice, not justice in terms of what theoretically ought, but justice in terms of what is felt to be just by all sorts of persons....."[2]. In fact industrial harmony developed in justice is said to be stronger than the one developed on good human relations. This situation of industrial harmony increases not only the effectiveness of the organization in producing goods and services but also the human development and satisfaction of persons in the organization.

Industrial harmony, however, does not mean that the interests of management and labour can be furthered indefinitely because at some stage or the other the interest of one group conflicts with those of the other and hence the society will have to control these interests and manage in such a way that the interests of all the groups are reasonably satisfied. It may be noted here that the management and unions have some interests in common like the preservation of the Organization, its jobs, and probably the preservation of the nature of the economic system. It is also to be realized that they, too, have certain common duties like the provision of cheap goods and services to the consumer. Thus, industrial harmony requires a community of reasonably responsible men so as to hold all the interests in balance and provide the maximum possible satisfaction to all the groups—particularly management, labour and the society at large. This emphasizes the fact that industrial harmony is a goal worth striving for in the long run. If the workers are discontented both with the material and other conditions of their life, it breeds conflicts. And if we allow the emergence and continuance of industrial conflicts, they might eventually destroy the very nature and structure of the economic system.

1. Homans George C., "*Industrial Harmony as a Goal,*" Industrial Conflict, edited by Arthur Kornhauser, Robert Dubin and Arthur M.Ross, McGraw-Hill Book company, Inc., New York, 1954 p. 49.

2. *Ibid.*, p.58.

It is true a society, where industrial conflict is suppressed by force, can also work. But in a democratic society this course of action cannot be thought of and the only possible method for the promotion of industrial harmony is by attacking the sources of discontent through appropriate steps. In fact the problem of preventing industrial conflict and keeping it within bounds and of maintaining Organizational harmony and morale are generally considered major responsibilities of the management. This line of action is based on the premise that productive efficiency and hence the profitability of business depends to a significant degree on the morale of work force. Productive efficiency in this context refers not only to the performance level of workers but to labour turnover, absenteeism, grievances, strikes and every other expression of apathy or hostility that interferes with the effectiveness of the organization.

Different programmes may be introduced to reduce the discontentment among workers. But what is required is not the introduction of a number of programmes to meet the different needs of workers, but the existence of "personnel spirit", in all these programmes. Every thing, the management does has its impact on human relationships within the Organization and hence makes for greater harmony or greater conflict. Hence, personnel-minded executives consider every policy and act from the stand point of how it will affect employees, whether it will make sense to them and be acceptable or whether it will make sense to them and be acceptable or whether it should be done in a different manner. Personnel practices are sure to succeed if this spirit prevails. One should proceed on the asumption that the interests of the employer and employee are fundamentally harmonious. It is true, serious strife may arise at times over wages and other terms of employement, but it can be prevented by more effective personnel administration including good treatment in respect of basic employment conditions. "It is now quite generally accepted that human relations programmes are never a substitute for sound economic relationships".[1]

2. Industrial Relations in India

There has been an acute necessity in India, especially during the post–independence period, to industrialize her economy in order to tackle the multifarious socio–economic problems. In the words of Pandit Jawaharlal Nehru, "the alternative (to industrialization) is to remain in a

1. Arthur Kornhouses, Robert Dubin and Arthur M. Ross, "*Alternative Roads Ahead*", Industrial Conflict, McGraw–Hill, Book Comany, Inc., New York, 1954, p. 511.

backward, underdeveloped, poverty–stricken and a weak country. We can't even retain our freedom without industrial growth".[1] Hence, one of the main goals of the Five Year Plans in India has been the rapid industrialization and more employment in secondary and territory industries. It is also viewed that "the first of the essential steps for building up an economically free and self–sustaining India is large–scale industrialization at a rapid and steady growth".[2]

With the attainment of independence, and with the launching of the planning era, serious and earnest efforts have been made towards rapid industrial and economic development of India. India has been "in the midst of an ambitious and critically important effort to raise the living standards of her people by integrated........"[3] industrial and economic development plans. The size of industrial labour in India has increased remarkably owing to rapid and planned industrial development. The increase in industrial labour led to the formation and development of trade unions and various social groups. It has also been recognized that management without labour would be sterile, and labour without management would be disorganized, ill–equipped and ineffective. It is realized that the concrete co-operation between labour and management is highly essential to the individual, organizational and national goals. The First Five Year Plan has clearly demonstrated the fact the "an economy organized for planned production and distribution, aiming at the realization of social justice and the welfare of masses, can function effectively only in an atmosphere of industrial peace."[4]

All these necessitate the maintenance of harmonious industrial relations so as to maintain higher productivity to fulfil the goals of the Five Year Plans in India. The investment in and the scope of industries in India have been growing plan after plan. Much of the success or failure of Indian Five Year Plans would be dependent on the maintenance of harmonious employee-employer relations. Frequent industrial conflicts

---

1. Report of the All India Congress Committee Session held at Avadi, January, 1955.
2. Sanjivayya, D., "*Labour Problems and Industrial Development in India,*" Oxford and IBH Publishing Co., New Delhi, 1970, p. 26.
3. Myers, Charles A and Kannappan Subbaiah, "*Industrial Relations in India,*" Asia Publishing House, Bombay, 1970, p.1.
4. Government of India, "*The First Five Year Plan*", Planning Commission, New Delhi, 1958,p.573.

not only affect the management and labour but also tend to impoverish the community as a whole. They lead to wastage, foment class-hatred, embitter mutual relations and inflict damage on the progress of the nation. They affect production and national income. They also clog the progress and development of the nation. Further, it is not an exaggeration to say that if we are successful in industry, the answer to class antagonisms and world conflicts will become easier.[1]

The objective of maintenance of industrial peace is not only to find ways and means to solve conflicts or to settle differences, but also to secure the unreserved co-operation of goodwill among different groups in industry with a view to driving their energies and interest towards economically viable, commercially feasible, financially profitable and socially desirable channels. It also aims at the development of a sense of mutual confidence, dependence and respect and, at the same time, encouraging them to come closer to each other for removing misunderstandings, redressing grievances, if any, in a peaceful atmosphere and with open mind, and fostering industrial pursuits for mutual benefit and social progress. But the maintenance of congenial industrial relations, particularly in a democratic society like ours, is not only a significant task but also a complicated one.

Industrial relations in India has passed through several stages. A number of factors—social, economic and political have—influenced industrial relations in India.[2]

During pre-independence days, the workers' wages and the working conditions were very poor.[3] The employers were in a commanding position. There were no trade unions and laws to protect the workers interest except the Employees and Workmen (Disputes) Act, 1860, which was used to settle wage disputes. At the end of World War-I, the industrial relations concept assumed a new dimension in the sense that workers resorted to violence and employers to lock-outs. There was an increase in strikes and disturbances during 1928-29. Ultimately the Central Government passed the long-awaited Trade Disputes Act of 1929, on the

---

1. King, W.L.M., "*Industry and Humanity*," The Macmillan Company of Canada Limited, Toronto, 1935,p.13.
2. Monappa, Arun, "*Industrial Relations*," Tata McGraw-Hill Book Company Ltd., New Delhi, 1987.p.9.
3. Giri, V.V., "*Labour Problems in Indian Industry*," Asia Publishing House, Bombay, 1972,p.81.

lines of the British Trade Disputes Bill of 1927, for the prevention and settlement of industrial disputes in India. The Bombay Government enacted the Bombay Industrial Relations Act by establishing an industrial court in order to prevent the industrial disputes prevailing in 1938.

Soon after the attainment of independence, the Government took a significant step in the field of industrial relations by enacting the Industrial Disputes Act, 1947, which not only provide for the establishment of permanent machinery for the settlement of industrial disputes, but also makes these awards binding and legally enforceable. An industrial conference was held in India in 1947, which made an appeal to workers and management in the form of an industrial harmony.

Immediately after independence (1947), a tripartite body, Indian Labour Conference (ILC), was set up to look into industrial relations problems in India. The objective behind setting up of the ILC was to establish co-operation among the Government, the employers and the trade unions.

An important characteristic feature of industrial relations in the post-Independence period was the change in the Government's attitude towards labour and their problems. Many labour laws were enacted to protect the interests of industrial workers during 1947 to 1956[1]. These covers many issues concerning labour, such as seniority, wage rates, paid holidays, disciplinary matters, social security and the like. The emphasis shifted from legal enactments to voluntary arrangements in 1957. "In fact the period between 1957 and 1965 can be regarded as an attempt to move away form legalism to voluntaryism which had dominated industrial relations in India."[2] The Code of Discipline was introduced in 1958. But, unfortunately, the Code of Discipline had a limited success as also a limited use.[3] Then the government thought of improving labour-management relations by legislation. The Government of India tried to structure the industrial relations machinery from plant level in the form of Works Committees.

1. *Ibid.*, p. 137.

2. Kaulgi, R.G., "*The Strategy and Tactics at the Bargaining Table*," Y.B. Bhonsle (ED) "Personnel Management; The Indian Scene." S. Chand & Co., New Delhi, 1977.

3. Government of India, "*Report of National Commission on Labour*", Ministry of Labour and Employment and Rehabilitation, New Delhi, 1966, p. 346.

The National Commission on Labour (NCL) was appointed by the Government in the year 1966 to look into labour matters and make recommendations, and submitted its report in 1969.

A National Apex Body (NAB) was set up in place of the tripartite ILC in consonance with the Government's 20-point economic programme in 1975 during the Internal Emergency. The National and State apex bodies were bipartite in composition. During the emergency, the discipline in industry was tightened. No unrest was observed. After the Emergency, the NAB was replaced by the ILC.

The Government appointed a tripartite committee on workers' participation in management and prepared a draft industrial relations bill (1978). The bill is for an understanding of the solution to some of the perennial industrial relations problems. But it never saw the light of the day.

At present, at the plant level, industrial relations has become highly regulated.[1] At present, Indian industrial relations, to some extent, are dominated by legalists as several labour laws have been passed. Many of the laws reflect the Government's socialistic orientation. The Government has also made efforts, in addition to management and union in several issues, to promote a bipartite collective bargaining situation. However, the industrial relations in India was characterized by violence during the late 1970s and early 1980s. Mounting cost of living, early settlement of disputes, and rising expectations were the main reasons for the violence during the period.

To meet the situation of industrial strife, the Government of India issued an ordinance to ban strikes on 26th July, 1981. The Essential Services Maintenance Act (ESMA) was also promulgated in July, 1981.

A sector-wise analysis of industrial disputes in India during the period 1985-1988 is presented in Table 1.1. It is clear form this table that the number of disputes both in public and private sectors declined during the period under study, except for a sharp rise in the year 1986 in private sector and in the year 1987 in public sector. But the number of workers involved increased form 385,000 to 1,007,000 in public sector during the period 1985 to 1987. However, it declined to 551,000 in 1988. This figure increased during the period 1985-87, but declined in 1988. This figure increased during the period 1985-87, but declined in 1988 in private sector also. The number of mandays lost recorded an increase during the

1. Monappa, Arun, *op. cit.* p. 11.

Table 1.1 : Industrial Disputes in India— Number and Consequences

	1985		*1986*		*1987*		*1988*	
	Public	*Private*	*Public*	*Private*	*Public*	*Private*	*Public*	*Private*
Number of Disputes	401	1354	389	1503	442	1357	269	664
Workers involved (*'000*)	385	694	678	967	1007	763	551	236
Mandays Lost (*'000*)	3002	26037	2572	30121	5237	30176	4808	13180
Wages Lost (*Rs. in crores*)	4.84	31.56	6.11	39.20	10.26	43.62	10.91	19.28
Production Loss (*Rs. in crores*)	29.06	345.46	40.06	783.52	108.52	531.43	42.49	359.76

Source : *Pocket Book of Labour statistics, 1989*, p. 85. Ministry of Labour, Government of India.

period 1985 to 1987 and declined in the immediate year both in public and private sectors. Though the number of mandays lost per dispute in public increased sharply from 7,480 to 17,870, it is less than that of private sector (19,220 in 1985 and 19,850 in 1988) during the period under study. The amount of wages lost owing to industrial disputes increased continuously from Rs. 4.84 crores to Rs. 10.91 crores in the public sector whilst it fluctuated between Rs. 43.62 crores and Rs. 19.28 crores during the period under study. This is mostly due to the loss of more number of mandays in the private sector than in the public sector. However, the amount of loss of production recorded an increase in 1986 in private sector and in 1987 in public sector. Thus it may be concluded that the industrial disputes and their consequences indicate unsound industrial relations situation in the country.

Unsound industrial relations may be caused by the absence of progressive personnel policies, programmes and practices, enlightened trade unions, ineffective functioning of collective bargaining and workers' participation in management.

3. Role of Workers' participation in Industrial Relations

Though harmonious industrial relations play a vital role in achieving plan targets, in our country the Government and employers could not get the unreserved co-operation of employees in maintaining congenial industrial relations in the country. Workers extend unreserved co-operation only when they are socially and psychologically involved in the entire process of management. A co-equal relationship between management and labour built around mutual trust and confidence plays a vital role in maintaining sound labour-management relations. The first step towards ensuring harmony between labour and management is to associate workers with the decision-making process. The system which involves the workers in the management process develops mutual trust and regard, develops employee commitment towards rendering whole-hearted co-operation to the management. Further, the system bridges the gulf created between mechanistic structures and human structures. In fact, this system enhances productivity and efficiency and fosters industrial harmony and human personality.[1] Workers' participation in management is the main subsystem of industrial relations which contributes to harmonious industrial relations.

Industrial relations situation in country has initiated setting up of various schemes of workers' participation within the framework of tripartite system of labour management relations in India in view of the significance of workers' participation in management.[2] The concept of participative management has great relevance in the industrial relations because it emerged as a measure for promoting harmony between labour and management. Consequently, the concept of workers' participation in management gained momentum in the country as a measure to improve industrial relations.

The objectives of workers' participation in management, according to the Government of India, include resolving industrial disputes, establishing industrial peace and harmony, and increasing productivity.[3]

Participation is the mental and emotional involvement of a person in a group-situation which encourages him to identify himself with group goals and share responsibilities with them.[4] It is considered to be a process by which employees can influence decision-making at various levels in an enterprise, either through their representatives on the board or in other

1. Sharma, B.R., "*Industrial Democracy : The Indian Experience*" Indian Journal of Industrial Relations, Vol. 2, January, 1987, p. 254.
2. Monappa, Arun, *op. cit.* p. 17.
3. Micheal, V.R., "*Industrial Relations and Workers' Involvement in Management,*" Himalaya Publishing House, Bombay, 1984, p. 204.
4. Davis, Keith, "Human Relations in Business" Tata McGraw-Hill Publications, New Delhi, 1962, p. 429.

participative forums. Extensive participation may lead to slower decision making, but it is possible to make decisions technically superior and carry them out without bitter conflicts between employees and management. Thus, though participation is not a perfect process, it is being used increasingly all over the world to supplement the contract relationship, as it provides a more rewarding work life and satisfies the legitimate expectations of employees.[1]

Social thinkers like Comte and Owen viewed that social justice could be achieved by encouraging workers' participation in management. From the point of view of social scientists, participative management is one of the tools of management where the emphasis is on the utility of a human approach.[2] The experiments of Blake, Mayo, Lewin and Likert popularized the belief that if workers are given opportunities to participate in the management process there could be positive gains to the Organizations effectiveness and morale.[3]

Profit maximization is not the sole objective of the Organizations. Peter Drucker advocated that industrial Organizations should have goals broader than profit-making and that they should substantially contribute to the realization of social goals and values.[4] In fact, the modern thinking on management is based on considering workers not merely as wage earners, but also as equal partners in the productive process. Democratic way of life being a goal of most of the societies, every Organization should try to achieve industrial democracy as "Political democracy will remain formalistic and legalistic if it is not supplemented by industrial democracy."[5]

Democratic way of life being a goal of most of the societies, every Organization should try to achieve industrial democracy as developments in the field of social sciences and political ideology concur with the concept of industrial democracy and particularly with workers, participation in management.

---

1. Trilateral commission, Collective Bargaining and Employee Participation in Western Europe, North America and Japan, New York, 1979.
2. Monappa, Arun, *op. cit.*, p 274.
3. *Ibid.*
4. Singh, B.P., et al. "Personnel Management and Industrial Relations", Dhanpat Rai & Sons, New Delhi, 1990, p. 424.
5. Giri, V.V., *op. cit.*, p. 15

Origin and Growth of Participative Management Schemes

Workers' participation in management (or co-determination) is not a new concept; it is as old as the institution of owners and workers.[1] With the industrialization and emergence of large industries, the importance of workers' participation in management, has been focused. A feeling of family spirit was in existence between the owner and worker where the units were small in the pre-industrial era.

Workers' Participation in Managements (WPM) can be classified into several forms. These are informative, consultative, associative, administrative and decisive participation.[2]

There is a sharing of information regarding production, finance, marketing, economic conditions etc., in informative participation. In consultative participation the issues relating to welfare facilities are discussed. In consultative participation the workers act in an advisory capacity and the decision is left to the management. In associative participation, the suggestions of the council are generally accepted by the management, and, if the decisions are unanimous, the managements is obliged to accept it and implement it. In administrative participation, the employees participate in administrative participation, the employees participate in administering the decisions taken already by the council. Finally, there is decisive participation, the highest form of participation where all matters, economic, financial, and administrative are brought under the purview of the councils and the decisions are taken collectively.

With the advent of the industrial revolution, the size of the enterprises increased, and along with it the numerical strength of the work force increased. And with the emergence of joint stock company type of Organization workers were neglected, eliminated from the process of working in conducive social environment and exploited for maximization of profits. Workers felt that since they had a much greater stake in their Organization, their interests should be protected. To counterbalance the power of the owners, workers organized themselves into unions and made the owners consider their various demands including point of view in the management of the enterprises. The owners, after recognizing the power of unions, gradually yielded to the demand of the

---

1. Viramani, B.R., "*Workers' Participation in Management: Some Experiences and Lessons.*" Macmillan Publishing House, Delhi, 1978, P.1.
2. Mhetras, V.G. "*Labour Participation in Management; An Experiment in Industrial Democracy in India,*" Manaktalas, Bombay 1966. pp. 18-21.

workers and negotiated with them on the aspects which directly affect the workers. Thus the employers yielded to pressures of the organized work force on occasions not because of change of heart but out of sheer compulsion.[1]

1. Philosophy and Practice—Global Scene

Viewed from the global perspective, the institutional culmination of the concept of workers' participation began with the establishment of joint committees of workers and management in several European countries towards the end of the World War-I.

Historically speaking, the earliest institutional form of participation was the Worker-Management Joint Committees which was set up in the British Municipal Undertakings following the recommendations of the Whitely Report submitted in 1916.[2] Subsequently, other countries such as the U.S.A., France, Sweden, West Germany, Poland, and Yugoslavia also made attempts to introduce scheme of workers' participation in management.

The initial interest in and enthusiasm about, participative management declined between the two world wars. After World War II, attention was paid to workers' participation in management through successive phases of tide and ebb in the subsequent decades. In most countries including the developing ones, a renewed push towards participatory management seems to have begun by the end of 1950s.[3]

The schemes of participation have assumed a variety of forms and structure indifferent countries. It is said that the cross country divergence relating to workers' participation in management has resulted largely from the difference in the political set up, governmental goals and values, economic and industrial structure and the aspect of socio-political culture of a particular country. However, a study of the workers' participation in management in various countries will provide the factors responsible for its development.

Joint Consultative Machinery in the United Kingdom

The idea of workers' participation in the United Kingdom (U.K.) began and grew with industrialization itself and was the result partly of

1. *Ibid.*, p. 2.
2. Mookherjee, Surya, "Joint Management Councils", Oxford and IBH Publishing Company, Pvt. Ltd., New Delhi, 1987, p. 1.
3. *Ibid.*, p. 2.

the compulsion of socialistic thought and partly due to the humanitarian attitude of some of the employers during the eighteenth century who realized the difficulties of the workers and tried to help them by holding informal discussions with representatives of workers.[1] Joint consultation and collective bargaining go together in the industrial relations system in the U.K. Joint Consultation (in the form of Joint Councils) in the British industries emerged with the recommendations of the Whitely Committee which was appointed by the Government.[2] As the term indicates it is consultative, and the areas of discussions was confined mostly to health, welfare and safety of the employees. Both the parties lost interest as the councils had no administrative powers.

Collective Bargaining in the U.K. is largely a decision-making process between the management and the trade unions. However, collective bargaining, which often proceeds with intensive power struggle, has a deteriorating effect on the industrial relations climate. The entire process is also based on mistrust, concealment of true introduction, misunderstanding and the use of negative pressure tactics.[3] In the U.K. both joint consultation and collective bargaining are not very successful.

Federal Republic of Germany

The development of workers' participation in management is not an exclusively post-war phenomenon as Works councils can be traced back to Bismark, and were developed in the early nineteenth century only in the erstwhile West Germany. But they were suppressed by the Nazis, and resurrected in the post-war period.[4] The revival came with the name Co-determination. The Government played a key role by legalizing the scheme, though it was introduced because of trade union demands. Though the scheme was initially introduced in coal and steel industries.[5] it was later extended to other industries.

Though the role of trade unions in the erstwhile West Germany is limited in co-determination, they play a major role in collective bargain-

1. Varandani, G., "*Workers' Participation in Management with Special Reference to India.*" Deep & Deep Publications, New Delhi, 1987, p. 45.
2. Rath, B.P. "*Workers' participation in Management -An Empirical Study.*" Unpublished Ph.D. Thesis, Berhampur University, Berhampur, 1985, p. 59
3. Virmani, B.P., *op.cit.*, p. 62.
4. Woodgate, Roger, "*Participation in West Germany: Another side of the Story.*" Personnel Management, February, 1979, pp. 38-43
5. Co-determination Act, 1951

ing process. Collective bargaining generally takes place at the industry level on issues like wages and working conditions, whereas co-determination and works councils take place at the enterprise level. Though it is said that the Works Councils cannot enter into the areas of collective bargaining, they have gradually enlarged their operations and encroached on the areas of collective bargaining in practice.[1]

The working of participative management schemes in the erstwhile West Germany presents a success story. The contributing factors for this are, effective and close communication between the works council and management, a co-operative work force and responsive trade unions,[2] and educated, enlightened and committed work force.[3] The scheme, though introduced and regulated by law, has taken deep roots and has become a way of life.[4] Both the parties i.e., workers and management, have achieved a standard of social partnership which does not suppress industrial conflict but provides a framework for settling them in civilized way.[5]

Yugoslavian Self-Management

The Yugoslavian system makes a distinction between workers' participation in management and the concept of self-management. The latter style gives complete control to workers to manage directly all aspects of industries through their representatives. The scheme introduced was a post-world War II development. The important bodies under self-management are: Workers' Council, Management Board, Director and Peoples' Committee.

Workers' council is the highest authority at the enterprise level. It consists of employees' representatives, elected for three years. The important functions of the council include planning, operations, financial management, and supervision of the work of the Management Board.[6]

---

1. Ramaswamy, E.A., and Rama Swamy Uma, "*Industry and Labour: An Introduction*," Oxford University Press, Delhi, 1981, p. 258.
2. Micheal, V.P., *op.cit.*, p. 210.
3. Schregle, Johannes, "*Co-determination in the Federal Republic of Germany: A comparative view*", International Labour Review, Vol. 117 No. 1, January-February, 1978. p. 88.
4. Viramani, B.R., *op.cit.*, pp. 49-50.
5. Vollmer, R.J., "*Industrial Relations in West Germany,*" Embassy of Federal Republic of West Germany, 1973.
6. Institute of Comparative Law, "*Constitution of Socialist Federal Republic of Yugoslavia,*" Institute of Comparative Law, Belgrade, 1963, p. 25.

The Management Board serves as the executive organ of the workers' council. The members of the board are elected from amongst the members of the workers' council for a term of one year, with the exception of the Director, who is only an ex-officio member.

The Director is at the apex level of the Organizational structure. He is selected by the council and local peoples' committee through competition for a term of four years. He is responsible for implementing the decisions of the council and board.[1]

The people's committee, comprising local people, plays an advisory role to the workers' council. The committee has a role in the appointment of director and also provides funds for the investment and payment of minimum wages.

Except these, the trade unions at the enterprise level have no direct role in the self-management but, they have the right to submit lists of candidates for workers' council and their approval is necessary for the council's decisions relating to wages, distribution of surplus etc. Inspite of this, trade unions are considered to be the basic Organization of the working class implementing and promoting self-management.[2]

Though self-management gives control to workers to manage all aspects, in practice, as found by Kolaja[3], workers are more concerned with day-to-day affairs and show little interest on economic aspects unless these affect them directly. The director takes most of the decisions.

Self-management based on the idea of social ownership has developed effective communication which keeps the workers informed of the day-to-day affairs. There is a sense of faith and belonging in the workers towards the system and the enterprise. These have contributed to making self-management a success and helped in preventing workers' exploitation.

The United States of America (U.S.A.)

Collective Bargaining is much widely used in the U.S.A. as the chief means for industrial democracy. Sturmthal observes; "the belief that

1. International Labour Office, "***Participation of workers in Decisions within undertakings***," International Labour Office, Geneva, 1969, p. 100.
2. Merinvik, Milos and Zynka, Simic, "***The Yugoslav Trade Unions***," Radnicka Stampa, Belgrade, 1970, p. 25.
3. Kolaja, J., "***Workers' Councils: The Yugoslav Experience***" Tavistock Publications, London, 1965.

collective bargaining is the main road towards industrial democracy, and that the collective agreement in its widest sense is its principal expression, is almost unchallenged by contemporary thought in the United States."[1]

A recent innovation in the U.S. enterprises is to develop co-operation which takes the form of joint management committees, production committees etc. Profit-sharing schemes as per Scanlon plan have become another means of fostering co-operation between workers and management. In addition, experiments on the quality of work-life emphasizing work-linked democracy are also going on. The idea behind these schemes are to extend collective bargaining beyond its traditional limits. The objective is to obtain benefits for both parties and not to bargain over the division of gains.[2]

Collective bargaining is the most effective way in which workers through their trade unions influence managerial decision-making. Most of the workers and trade unions are not interested in formal participation in management.[3] The presence of mutual trust and dependence, effective communication between the parties and single, strong, democratic and enlightened trade union with an enlightened work force have greatly contributed to the success of the American style of industrial democracy.

To sum up, the term participative management differs from country to country. The form and content also vary from country to country based on the social, political and economic mileu of a country.

2. Indian Perspective

In India, isolated instances of worker participation can be found even as early as 1920 in the form of informal joint consultation in the cotton textile industry. The employers of textile industry started mill committees to discuss the grievances of the workers. But the management did not accept the committee as spokesmen on behalf of emerging trade

1. Stumthal Adolf F., "*Workers' Participation in Management: A Review of United States Experience*," IILS Bulletin, June, 1969, p. 160.
2. Bett, William, L.Jr., and Weinberg, William, "*Labour Management co-operation Today*" Harvard Business Review, January-February, 1978, pp. 96-104.
3. "*We do not seek to be a partner in Management*" was the remark made by Thomas Donahue to the International Conference on Trends in Industrial and Labour Relations, Montreal, Canada, May 26, 1976. Quoted by Mills, Ted, "*Europe's Industrial Democracy: An American Response*," Harvard Business Review, November-December, 1978, pp. 143-152.

unions, the existence of which they preferred to ignore.[1] Though such consultation was of a rudimentary type,[2] yet it was significant as it was the first of its kind in the country.

Works committees were constituted by the Government in printing presses and railways to promote harmonious relations after the World War 1.[3] During the same period such committees were formed in the Tata Iron and Steel Company, Jamshedpur.[4]

In the same year, a permanent arbitration Board a joint body to settle unresolved disputes was set up in the Ahmedabad Cotton Textile Industry under the inspiration of Mahatma Gandhi, who also acted as the labour representative on the Arbitration Board.[5]

Although the scope of mutual consultation was confined largely to the grievances of workers, the Ahmedabad agreement may be regarded as a milestone in the history of the joint consultation in our country.[6] The Royal Commission on Labour opined that `the system is admirable in its intention and had a substantial measure of success.'[7]

Joint Committees of workers and management were formed form 1922 onwards in Bengal, Madras and other states. After reviewing the performance of such committees, the Royal Commission on Labour observed that 'some committees have been successful and there are probably few that have been without use, but generally speaking the results achieved have been disappointing.[8] The reasons for this is the lack of clarity with the management and trade unions. The commission recommended formation of works committees with the view that if they

1. Pearse, Arnos, "*The Cotton Industry of India*" Manchester, 1930.
2. Pylee M.V., "*Workers' Participation in Management: Myth and Reality,*" N.V. Pub!ications, Delhi, 1975, p. 23.
3. Government of India, Report of Royal Commission on Labour in India, New Delhi, 1931, p. 331.
4. Tata Steel, "*Concept of Working together,*" 1988, p. 11.
5. The Employees Federation of India, "*Worker Participation in Management,*" Monograph, 1971, p. 2.
6. Pande, R.S., "*The Position and Responsibilities of the Personnel Department Inside Undertakings,*" Mimeograph, Labour Management Relations Series No. 7, I.L.O., Geneva, 1960.
7. Government of India, "*Report of the Royal Commission on Labour in India.*" *op.cit.*, 337.
8. *Ibid.*, p. 336.

were given proper encouragement and past errors were avoided, these committees could play a useful role in the Indian Industrial Relations System[1].

The Commission also recommended establishment of a joint machinery exclusively for settlement of disputes. However, no effective steps were taken to implement these recommendations.

The more important development in the field came in the year 1947 with the enactment of the Industrial disputes Act, which required the setting up of works committees in all undertakings employing 100 or more workers. The Central Government, by an order issued in May, 1948, required the establishment of works committees in major ports, required the establishment of works committees in major ports, mines, oil fields and other Central Government undertakings. The First Five Year Plan (1951-56) also called for the construction of joint committees for consultations at all levels and reiterated the Government's faith in the works committee. It stated that works committee for the settlement of differences on the spot between the workers and the management is the key of the system of industrial relations as conceived in this plan."[2]

The Second five Year Plan (1956-61), however, admitted indirectly that the worked committee had not been much of a success. It is clear from the statement that "Experience has shown that a major hindrance in the way of effective functioning of works committees is the lack of a clear cut demarcation between their responsibilities, and the responsibilities operating in the field."[3] The Second Five Year Plan highlighted the importance of workers' participation for the purpose of promoting productivity satisfying the workers urge for self expression and better understanding their role and for industrial peace. The plan recommended setting up of joint councils with representatives from management and workers.[4] Some Organizations like TISCO and Indian Aluminium Company constituted joint councils prior to the Second five Year Plan. Nabagobal Das Felt that the Scheme envisaged by the plan was considered to be rather vague and both employers and workers spoke apprehensively about the likely impact of the scheme on labour management relations.[5]

---

1. *Ibid.*, p. 342.
2. Government of India, *'The First Five Year Plan.' op.cit.*, p. 573.
3. Government of India, "*The Second Five Year Plan,*" Manager of Publications, 1956, Delhi, p. 576.
4. *Ibid.*, p. 49.
5. Das, Nabagopal, "*Experiments in Industrial Democracy*". Asia Publishing House, Bombay, 1964, p. 130.

As the proposed introduction of the scheme through joint councils of management was relatively a new idea in which the country had little experience, the Government of India sent abroad a Study Group in 1956 to understand the many problems in detail in respect of workers' participation in management. The group comprised representatives from the government, trade unions, and the employers. The study group, in their report suggested a scheme of workers' participation in management which was almost similar to the British system of Joint Management Councils and Committees (JMCs).[1]

The report of the study group was considered by the 15th session of the Indian Labour Conference held in July, 1957. The list of functions for the JMCs were finalized in 1957 under three heads viz., consultative, information sharing and administrative. A novel feature of the scheme has been that it has bot been made statutory and the tripartite agreement formed the sole basis for the introduction of this voluntary scheme.[2]

The ILC appointed a tripartite sub-committee which recommended the introduction of the scheme in such Organizations as have more than 500 workers, a strong trade union, a fair record of industrial relations and readiness of the parties to try out the experiment. The committee also recommended that the plant level council should form with an equal membership form the management and the workers side.

A seminar was organized by the Union Labour Ministry in February, 1958, to discuss the constitution, functions and administrative problems connected with the JMCs. Initially 53 enterprises (21 from public sector and 32 from private sector) were selected for the experiment, and the target was raised in later years to 150. However, the country could never achieve the target.[3] Further, of the 53 units initially selected 30 showed willingness, yet only 11 constituted the councils.[4] Thus, the growth of the JMCs from the beginning was slow.

---

1. Government of India, "*Report of the Study group on Workers' Participation in management*," New Delhi, 1957, p. 130.
2. Rath, G.C., and Murthy, B.S., "*Participative Management: The Indian Experience*," the Indian Journal of Social Work, Vol. XXXVI, no. 1, April 1975, pp. 37-47.
3. Chaterjee, N.N., "Management of Personnel in Indian enterprises." Allied Book Agency, Calcutta, 1986, p. 530.
4. Sheth, N.R. "Joint Management Councils, problems and Prospects," Shri Ram Centre for Industrial Relations and Human Resources, Delhi, 1972, p. 9.

The Ministry of Labour organized a second seminar in March, 1960, to review the experiences and to examine the difficulties in the way of further progress. The participants found that the exact nature and functions had not been formed.

Considering all these opinions, the Third Five Year Plan (1961-66), again re-affirming the value of JMCs in strengthening the industrial relations situation in the nation, recommended the setting up of JMCs in all industrial undertakings found suitable for the purpose so that, in due course of time, the scheme might become a normal feature of the industrial system.[1] The Fourth Five Year Plan urged the extension of workers' participation on the public sector departmental undertakings and emphasized its importance as an essential functional link in the structure of industrial relations[2].

Though the number of JMCs increased from 23 in 1958 to 147 in 1967[3], it did not become main characteristic feature of the Indian industrial relations system. It is observed that the JMCs were successful in the units where labour-management relations were cordial, viz., The Tata Iron and Steal Company Ltd. (TISCO)[4] and Indian aluminium works at Belur.[5] In toto the JMC was an even more resounding failure than the works committee had been.[6]

Scheme of Worker Directors

The worker directors' scheme was introduced by some public enterprises and 14 commercial banks in 1970, in response to the Governments' directive. The scheme of workers' directors did not show any impact on the decision making process because of their lack of familiarity

1. Government of India, "Third Five Year Plan." Manager of Publications, Delhi, 1961.
2. Government of India, "Fourth Five Year Plan," Manager of Publications, Delhi, 1969.
3. Government of India, Ministry of Labour, Employment and Rehabilitation, "Quarterly Review of the Working of the Joint Management Council," The author (unpublished), New Delhi.
4. Government of India, Ministry of Labour, "Management Consultation and Co-operation in the Tata Iron and Steel Industry," The Author, New Delhi, 1958.
5. Xavier Labour relations institute, The Belur report - a Case Study, The Author, Jamshedpur, 1958 (Mimeograph).
6. Ramaswamy, E.A., and Ramaswamy Uma., op.cit., p. 265.

with the principles and practice of management and also owing to the internal conflicts between their role as union leader and part of top management as member of the board. As such, the scheme could not make much head away.

National emergency and Participative Management

During the Internal Emergency in 1975, the Government of India announced a new scheme of workers' participation in management as a part of the 20-Point Economic Programme. The councils and joint councils in the manufacturing and mining establishments employing more than 500 persons in private, co-operative and public sectors including departmentally run units. The Constitution of India was amended during the very period through the 44th amendment[1] which was made the 42nd Amendment Act of 1976, incorporating the principles of workers' participation in the directive Principles of State Policy.

The membership of these councils (consisting of not more than 12 in the case of shop council) is divided equally between management and workers. The tenure of each council is two years and decisions are taken on the basis of consensus, which will be implemented within a month. The workers' representatives are from among the workers actively engaged in the department of the enterprise, while the chairman of a shop council is the nominee of the management. The chief executive of the enterprise is the chairman of the joint council. The Vice-chairman in both cases is from among the worker members. These councils are meant to assist the management in achieving monthly/yearly production targets, improving production and productivity, elimination of wastage, improving safety, health, and welfare measures, and ensuring discipline and a two-way communication between the labour and the management.

The Report of Ministry of Labour for 1977-78 said that the scheme had helped in improving production, productivity and overall efficiency as well as the industrial relations situation in the industries. It further reported that the scheme was in operation in 1,400 units out of the total required number of 1,795 units.[2] the Central Government in January,

1. Article 43 of the Indian Constitution as amended by the 42nd amendment Act, of 1976 provided for Article 43 'A' which read as: 'That the State shall take steps by suitable legislation or in any other way, to secure the participation of workers in the management of undertakings, establishments or other Organizations engaged in any industry.

2. Rath, B.P., *op.cit.*, p. 92.

1977, extended this scheme to other units of service and commercial Organization which employ 100 or more workmen.

Both the schemes functioned effectively in improving productivity and industrial relations climate. But after the lifting of the Emergency and change in the Government, the scheme suddenly lost its effectiveness.[1] Thus the present scheme also met with the same fate as the two earlier schemes viz., works committee and joint management councils, did.

The new Government, in 1977, tried to give a fresh look to the various schemes of participation which were in operation as on that date. The Government constituted a 21-member committee headed by the Central Labour Minister to examine the existing scheme and recommend a comprehensive scheme of participation. The Committee, felt that "as experience of voluntary schemes of participative management in the past had not been very happy, it was essential to introduce the scheme through legislation."[2] The committee also suggested that details of a three-tier system of participation in undertakings employing 500 or more workers (to be elected through secret ballot), with parity representation on the shop level and plant level. There was, however, no unanimity regarding the extent of employee representation at the corporate level[3].

Though the new Government at the Centre took Office in 1980, it reiterated the strengthening of the participative management schemes in late 1983. The scheme proposed by Ministry of Labour would be voluntary, covering all central public sector undertakings except those that are specifically exempted by the administrative machinery or department concerned in consultation with the Department of Labour. This scheme also did not show any progress during the years. The National Front Government at the center convened a national seminar in January, 1990, and elicited the views of different sections of Rajya Sabha in 1990. The Bill is intended to make the scheme statutory and implement the scheme in all sincerity. But the bill has not yet taken the form of a legislation. However, both public and private sector industries in India introduced the scheme of workers' participation in Management.

India adopted the mixed economic system in pursuit of the socialistic pattern of society. The Government controls the public sector. Public

---

1. *Ibid.*
2. Government of India, Report of the Committee (Chairman: Ravindravarma) on workers' participation in Management and Equality, Sep. 1977.
3. *Ibid.*

sector plays the most crucial role by instituting core industry like steel, coal, heavy electricals, electronics. petro chemicals etc., and the private sector concentrates on other industries. Thus the roles of public and private sectors in a mixed economy are complimentary to each other.

The Report of the Ministry of Labour for 1977-78 stated that about 688 units in private sector in various states introduced various schemes of participative management. But the Government of India, in their survey, found that the participative management schemes have been functioning successfully in Tata Iron and steel company (One of the largest private sector industries in the country) than in any other private sector industry in the country.[1] In fact TISCO introduced the schemes of WPM much before the schemes introduced by the Government of India in 1919. Out of the 244 operational public sector undertakings, only 238 have implemented various schemes of participative mangement.[2]

Participative management in some of the public sector undertaking, for example Bharat Heavy Electricals Limited[3] have provided an appropriate forum for effective communication, and management have unreservedly furnished all facts and information sought for, the unions have responded by moderating their enthusiasm and exercising reasonable restraint in demanding information, disclosure of which could be detrimental to the interest of the Organization.

Thus it is felt that the functioning of the participative management is not satisfactory in most of the public and private sectors in the country owing to various reasons. The most important among them is non-voluntary involvement of the member in the participative forums. This factor led to the introduction of Quality Circles in various industries as a supplementary measure to the schemes of workers' participation in management.

Quality Circles—An Evolutionary Approach

Quality Circle is a participative management system in which workers voluntarily make suggestions and improvements for the better-

---

1. Government of India, "*Management Consultation and Co-operation in the Tata Iron and Steel company.*" *op.cit.*

2. Rai, Aparna and Agarwal D.C., "*Labour relations in Public Sector Enterprises,*" Journal of Public Enterprises, Vol. 6, Np. 10, June, 1991, pp. 88-96.

3. Gangadhara Rao, M., et. al., "*Human Resources Management in Public Sector,*" Himalaya Publishing House, Bombay, 1991, p. 128.

ment of the company.[1] According to the International Association of Quality Circles, Quality Circle is a "group of factory workers from the same work area who usually meet for an hour each week to discuss their quality problems, investigate causes, recommend solutions, and take corrective actions when authority is in their purview."[2] The Quality Circle Forum of India defined the term keeping in view the essence of the philosophy as it originated in Japan as, "a small group of employees in the same work area or doing similar type of work who voluntarily meet regularly for about an hour every week to identify, analyze and resolve the work-related problems, leading to improvement in their total performance and enrichment of their work life."[3]

As is well known, after the ravages of the World War II, Japan was frantic to put its industries back on their feet, and for that purpose it sought the assistance of American Management experts to help it in this direction. Dr. Deming, of the U.S.A. taught the Japanese statistical, delivered a series of lectures on management of quality, to different Organizations in Japan. While such a timely help from the Americans did aid the Japanese in adopting modern management tools for improving their industries, they realized that in order to dispelled the long-standing image of Japanese goods being shoddy and cheap, they had to evolve their own techniques to have an edge over Western products and thus be competitive in the international market.

Such an anxiety for their very survival prompted the Japanese to organize massive training to all sections of employees on Quality and Productivity. It was then that they realized that the workers, given the opportunity, are capable of using their brain power and creativity for identifying problems, resolving them and ensuring the implementation of their own recommendations voluntarily. They believed that it is the worker who knows best what the problems in his area are and how best they could be solved. The worker could be motivated to take active interest in bringing about improvements in his work only if he has a say in decisions affecting him.

It was thus that in 1962, the first Quality Circle was launched in Japan under the leadership of Prof. ISHIKAWA.

---

1. Sud Ingle, "*Quality Circles Master Guide, Increasing Productivity with People Power*," Prentice-Hall of India Pvt. Ltd., New Delhi, 1985, p. 16.
2. Ibid.
3. Quality Circle Forum of India, "*Training for Quality Circles*" QCFI, Secunderabad, 1984, p. 7.

The concept soon spread all over Japan and became a movement which has now more than ten million workers involved in Quality Circles. Now over forty countries in the world including the USA, the UK, Phillipines, Australia, Korea, Sweden and India are operating Quality Circles.

1. Philosophy of Quality Circles

The Philosophy of Quality Circles is built around the following:

1. Contribute to the improvement and development of the enterprise.
2. Respect humanity and build a happy bright work-shop where
   a. People are not treated as part of machinery, but as human beings engaged in meaningful jobs and exposing their full potential;
   b) People use their wisdom and creatively in work they are engaged in;
   c) People develop their ability through an opportunity to use their brains;
   d) People are not isolated from each other and act as a group creating harmonious human relations based on the bonds of brotherhood in the work-shop;
   e) People mutually educate themselves by sharing an experience.
   f) People are given due recognition by all.
3. Display human capabilities fully and eventually draw out infinite possibilities.
4. It promotes job involvement and participation.
5. In short, it is a people building philosophy.

The Organization of Quality Circles is shown in Fig.1.1. It consists of Non-Members, Member, Leader/Deputy Leader, Facilitator, Steering Committee, Top Management, and Co-ordinating agency.

At base a quality Circles (QC) embraces even the non-members. This is based on the belief that once the recommendation of Q C. are ready to be implemented, everyone in the Organization is required to abide by them. In that sense, even the non-members would render a part of the process.

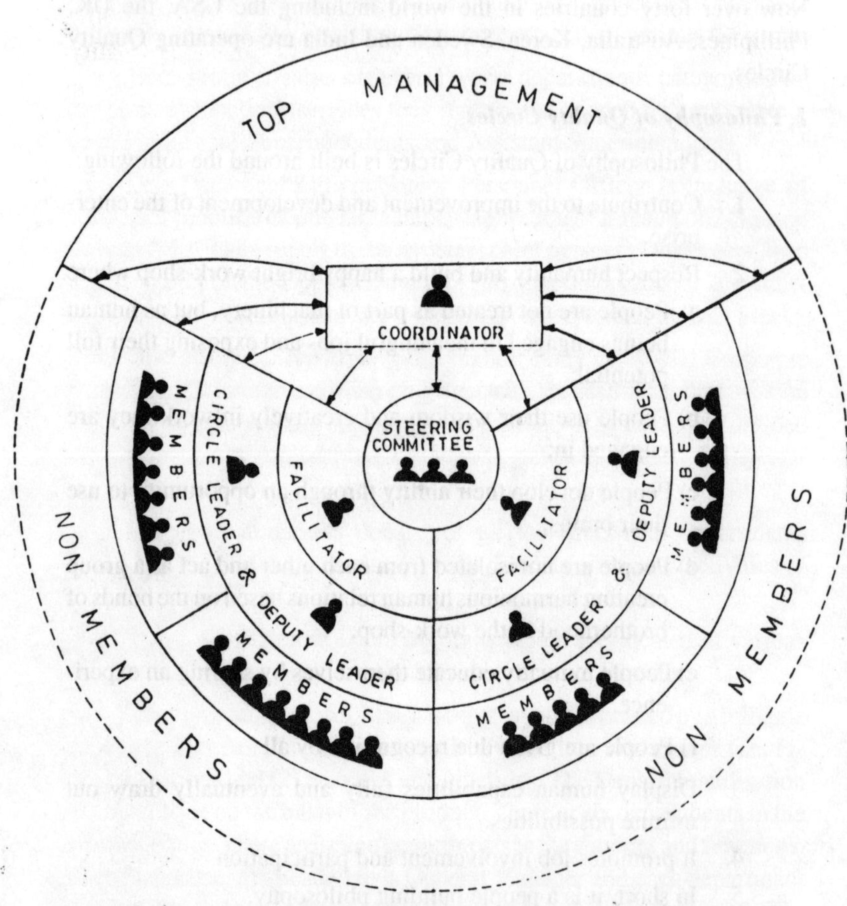

Fig. 1.1
Structure of Quality Circles

The quality circle consists of four to ten members who are drawn from the same work area and doing similar work, in order to ensure cohesiveness in identifying and solving problems. They meet regularly for about an hour every week to discuss and analyze various issues. Membership is strictly voluntary and their collective objective is to strive for the highest standards or performance of their quality circles.

The leader is either a regular work leader or a competent circle member chosen by the members themselves. He guides, trains the other members with the help of facilitator and maintains a high degree of cohesiveness by involving every member.

The facilitator is usually a senior officer nominated by the management; he is in-charge of a shop or department. As management's representative, he amply demonstrates the support, faith and conviction of the management of the concept; he primarily solves, interfaces problems between circles and other functional areas, and reports to the steering committee about effectiveness or otherwise of the QC in his area, and takes corrective actions to revitalize inactive quality circles. It is of utmost importance that a facilitator should be committed to a participative style of management.

The steering committee, which comprises representatives of all major functions, is responsible for establishing objectives and resources, and it gives thrust by promoting QCs as a way of life.

The `Top' management is meant to be represented by the Chairman and Managing Director, Directors, Chief Executives. They are expected to lend total philosophy and activities of the quality circles without the faith and commitment, support and encouragement from this top level. The quality circle activities cannot be deemed to have complete support for the programme. To look after the activities of quality circle (i.e., convening the steering committee meetings, arranging management presentations, formulating budgets and disseminating relevant information, each Organization normally sets up a separate agency called Co-ordinating Agency with the responsibility of co-ordination.

2. Quality Circles in India

Dwivedi observes that, historically, Gun Mandals (Quality Circles) have been used in different social, religious and political settings since the dawn of Indian civilization to enhance sattivic qualities (i.e./urge for excellence and knowledge, concern for others' interests, trust and confidence self-actualization etc.,) and minimize rajasic (urge for economic resources, authority and power, concern for personal interests, restlessness, and tension, craze for ego-inflation etc.) and tamasic qualities (i.e. proneness to error, indolence and wickedness, urge to exploit and damage others, distrust, loss of self identity etc.). Notwithstanding the roots of quality circles in Indian culture and their immense possibilities for integrating the individuals and the Organization through development of sattivic qualities in human system, Indian managers did not use them in industrial Organizations till the seventies.[1]

In 1980 Mr. Udpa, the then General Manager, Bharat Heavy Electricals Limited (B.H.E.L.) Hyderabad Unit, during one of his business visits to Japan, came to know about the operation of the quality circles in that country. He had discussions with Prof. Shin Miura of Tamagawa University on the subject, which helped him to gain a general insight into the philosophy and working of quality circles in Japan.

Mr. Udpa after returning to India, held discussions with different sections of the executives in BHEL on the methodology to be adopted. For the purpose, two work areas with dissimilar activities were initially selected for launching the experiment, one in production and another in service. The management clarified the queries raised by the workers, and the first quality circle was launched on an experimental basis in November, 1980. About the functioning of the circles, Udpa says: "It is gratifying to note the keen interest that the workers started taking part in the working of quality circles. Although they were new to the concept, they followed the principle without any difficulty." The members of quality circles in the Organization were able to make a top management presentation[2] within the three months of the formation of first five quality circles (which were formed in November, 1980 and formally inaugurated on 5th January, 1981).[3] spontaneous enthusiasm developed as the news spread about the success of these quality circles and activity started in other areas as well. Thus by the end of 1988-89, 16,569 circles were started in BHEL.

---

1. Dwivedi, R.S. "*Effectiveness of Quality Circles and its Determinants in a large Industrial Organization in India,*" Indian Journal of Industrial relations, Vol. 22, No. 4, April, 1987, p. 355.

2. Top Management Presentation is the culmination of a Circles' Project Study. The recommended solution of the selected Problem would be more effective and purposeful if the presentation is made in a systematic way. These case studies would also serve as effective educational tools in future.

3. Udpa S. R., "*Quality Circles in India,*" Tata McGraw-Hill Publishing Company, New Delhi, 1982, p. 27.

After hearing about the success of quality circles in BHEL, many Organizations showed interest. Then the establishment of a non-profit national body was found necessary to give all information regarding quality circles' activities within the country and abroad and to organize seminars/workshops as well as training programmes for the propagation of quality circles in the rest of the country. As a result, a non-profit body Quality Circle Forum of India (QCFI) was formed in 1982. The QCFI organizes seminars, workshops, conferences etc., to propagate the concept of quality circles and to offer training facilities. Different public and private sector Organizations operate quality circles viz., The Tata Iron and Steel Company Ltd., Hyderabad Allwyn, Bajaj Auto, Bharat Electronics Limited, Electronics Corporation of India Ltd., Air India., Shri Ram Fibers, The Tata Engineering and Loco motives company Limited, National Textile Corporation, Apollo Hospitals etc. The quality circles are called differently in various organizations viz., Employee Participation Circles and Small Group Activities. One of the spin-off benefits the quality circle movement has brought about is the attitudinal changes seen at all levels in the participating companies.[1]

Conclusion

India cannot afford work stoppages due to industrial disputes as it has to industrialize her economy based on Five Year Plans. Further attainment of plan targets is possible with the maximum contribution of human resources to the organizational goals. But the industrial relations situation in the country is not conducive to the attainment of organizational goals and thereby plan targets. Workers' participation in management is expected to play a vital role not only in the maintenance of harmonious industrial relations but to the successful achievement of goals of individual workers, Organization and the country at large. Though the philosophy and practice of workers' participation in management varies slightly from country to country, its basic objective is to involve the workers in the process of decision–making and management with a view to securing their contribution to the development of organization and individual. But, the schemes of participative management in India suffer from structural defects like requirements of involuntary participation of the workers, absence of support of the top management and absence of legal sanction for implementation of decisions taken in the meetings of workers' participation in management. Hence, it is suggested

1. Madhurendra K. Varma, "*Quality Circle–A Catalyst for Motivation,*" Indian Management, February, 1988, p. 33.

that the Government and Management should take necessary steps to modify the structure of the workers' participation in management in such a way that these basic structural defects are rooted out.

The defect of involuntary participation gave birth to a new concept called quality circles. Quality circle is relatively of recent origin, first experimented in Japan. The basic advantage of this technique over workers' participation in management is voluntary association and participation of members in identifying, analyzing the work related problems and finding out the solutions. The scheme is expected to be complimentary to workers' participation in management and contribute more effectively than participative management to the goals of individual workers and the organization.

The Present Study

Significance of the Study

India cannot escape from massive industrialization in veiw of the galloping growth of population and the inability of the agriculture sector to meet the needs of the rising population, to raise the gross national product and the percapita of the people, to increase the living standards, and to meet the varying needs of th people. Further, the agriculture sector in these days depends heavily on the industrial sector both for its inputs and disposal of its output. It is needless to overmphasise industrialisation as India would not have been able to develop to its present stage of economic growth without the industrial progress.

The massive industrialisation in India through setting up of large and gigantic industries in the core sector would not be as it is today but for the contribution of the public sector. A close exemination of the industrial development in India reveals that the institution of public sector plays a crucial and strategic role in the development of all categories of industries. In fact, the public sector is created to launch and control large capital intensive industries, industries involving high risk of return and low rate of profitability. Public sector indsutries are expected to render social responsibilites like fertilizers, petro-chemicals, steel, coal, railways, posts and telegraphs, engineering, transport etc. Public sector in India before the 1950s confined its activities only to the areas of railways, posts and telegraphs, defence factories etc. But today it covers a wide range of activities consisting of manufacturing sector, service sector commercial sector and so on. The number of central public sector undertakings increased from 5 to 231,[1] and their capital went up from Rs. 290 millions to Rs. 712,290 millions[2] during 1951 to 1988. Employment increased from 20.90 lakhs to 31.96 lakhs[3] during the period 1960-61 to 1980-81. The share of public enterprise on the total capital stock is 37.00 per cent.[4] The share of investment of manufacturing industries in the total capital of public enterprises is 76.00 per cent[5] in 1986-87.

The engineering industry occupies a premirer position as one of the major instruments of the economic development of the country. The share of engineering group in investment is 5.1 per cent.[6] It provided employment to about 16.00 lakh people.[7] There are about 5,000 manaufacturing units in the industry with the estimated gross annual production value of Rs. 30,000 millions as on 31st March, 1990.[8] It produces a wide variey of goods including heavy electrical equipment, heavy machine tools, industrial machinery etc. Among the public sector enginnering units, the Bharat Heavy Electricals Limited (BHEL) plays a significant role. It is engaged in the production of specialised heavy electrical equipment like power transformers, industrial traction motors etc. BHEL is the sixth[9] largest profit-making public sector undertaking in the country. It is recognised as a progressive employer in maintaining sound industrial relations.[10]

Private sector industries in India include individual enterprises was completely responsible for economic development in India before the 1950s, still the private sector plays a dominant role in India's industrial development. The Government allotted specific goals and role to the private sector in its successive industrial policy resolutions. In fact, the

1. Bureau of Public Enterprises. 1987-88, p. 230.
2. *Ibid.*
3. Government of India *"Pocket Book of Labour and Economic Survey","* Ministry of Labour, 1981-82.
4. Datt, Ruddar and Sundharam, K.P.M., "*Indian economy,*" S. Chand & Co. (P) Ltd., New Delhi, 1989, p. 154.
5. *Ibid.*
6. *Ibid.*, p. 155.
7. Sivayya, K.V., and Das, V.B.M., "Indian Industrial Economy" S.Chand & Co. (P) Ltd., Delhi, 1990, p. 470.
8. *Ibid.*
9. Gangadhara Rao, M., et. al. op.cit. p. 12.
10. BHEL, Personnel Mannual.

Government appreciated the dynamism of the private sector for its contributions to the gross domestic product and economic development. The number of private sector industries increased from 29,283 to 1,33,056.[1] Its capital rose up from 10,050 millions to 71,740 millions during the period 1957 to 1986.[2] contribution of the private sector to the net domestic product was 75.5 per cent[3] in the year 1984-85. It provides employment to 93.00 per cent[4] of the people working in the corporate sector. Normally, private sector industries concentrate on consumer goods like sugar, paper, cement, electronics, light engineering goods etc. But certain large industries produce steel and engineering products. The Tata Iron and steel Company Ltd. (TISCO) and the Tata Engineering and Locomotive Company Ltd. (TELCO) dominate in the critical, strategic and core industries within the private sectors. Thus, among the private sector industries, TISCO plays a dominant role. Further, it occupies the first place[5] in private sector indsutries in the country in respect of turnover. It is recognised as one of the best model and progressive employers in the country.[6] It is worthy to quote that there has been no industrial conflict in TISCO during the last forty years.[7]

The above analysis indicates that BHEL—the six among the top ten profit- earning public sector undertakings in the country did not see any major sign of industrial unrest during the period 1982-83 and 1988-89. This is a core manufacturing industry in the public sector in the country. The industry in private sector with similar characteristics *i.e.*, absence of industrial conflicts during 1982-83 to 1988-89 and a core and manufacturing industry, is the Tata Iron and Steel Company, Jamshedpur. Moreover, TISCO has not experinced any major industrial conflicts during the last forty years. This might be due to efficient management of human resources and maintenance of industrial relations on effective and democratic lines. Workers' participation in management, a major scheme of industrial democracy, may have played a pivotal role in these two

---

1. Datt, Ruddar and Sundharam, K.P.M., *op.cit*., p. 177.
2. *Ibid.*
3. *Ibid.*
4. *Ibid.*
5. Business India, Sept. 30 - Oct. 13, 1991, p. 56.
6. Tata Steel, "*Concept of Working Together*", Personnel Division, TISCO, Jamshedpur, 1988, p. 10.
7. *Ibid.*

industrial units in maintaining sound industrial relations. Keeping this background in view, it is felt that a study of workers' participation in management in these two units will be of great value.

The Industrial Units under Study

1. Profile and Progress

(a) Profile and Progress of BHEL

The electrical power availability at the time of our Independence was very low and around 1700 MW[1], mostly from hydro sources. Since power is a vital input to industry and agriculture, electrical power development was given a very high importance in successive five year plans. The Government of India realised that it is absolutely necessary to have indigenous manufacturing facilities for accelerating the availability of electrical power.

Heavy Electricals (India) Limited (HE(I) LTD.) was set up in Bhopal in 1955 with a view to achieving self-sufficiency in industrial products and power equipment which has been vital for the industrialisation of the country. Subsequently, at the time of formulation of the Third Five Year Plan, it was realised that one plant alone would not be able to cater to the requirements of power plant additions in the country. A separate company called Bharat Heavy Electricals Limited (BHEL) was formed in 1964 to start three more plants and to manufacture equipment for power plants, at Hardwar, Hyderabad, and Trichy. In 1974 both Heavy Electricals (India) Limited and Bharat Heavy Electricals Ltd., merged, emerging as the present BHEL, the largest engineering and manufacturing organisation of its kind in India. It ranks among the 500 big companies in the world.[2] And it also ranks among the top 12 power equipment manufacturers in the world.[3] It has 13 manufacturing divisions which are located in Bhopal, Hardwar, Jhansi, Bangalore, Trichy, Jagdishpur, Rudrapur, Goindwal, Ranipet and Hyderabad and a number of service divisions all over the country. BHEL has the capability to offer a variety of high technology equipment required for thermal, hydro and nuclear power plants, transmission and transportation sectors, electronics and industry sectors and also non- conventional energy systems, extending further into services of

1. Tallur, N.S., "*Experiences in Human resources Development at BHEL,*" HRD Centre, BHEL, Hyderabad, 1989, p. 3.
2. Survey conducted by Fortune, U.S.A., 1989.

undertaking, turnkey projects in the above areas.Out of 59,008 MW commissioned upto March, 1989 in India, BHEL's share is around 62.7 per cent.[1]

BHEL has recorded a steady growth over the past years. The capital outlay in the Year 1977-78 was Rs. 4,345.5 millions and it increased to 15,470.20 millions in 1989-90.[2] The turnover in the years 1982-83 was Rs. 11,790 millions which increased to Rs. 28,500 millions in 1989-90[3]. The company has a workforce of 74,436[4] in 1989-90. BHEL is the first public sector undertaking to secure the best industrial relations award for the year 1983.[5]

The Heavy Power Equipment Plant (HPEP) at Hyderabad (Ramachandrapurm was established under the farmework of the Indo-Czechoslovakian economic agreement. The plant was set up for manufacture of 60 and 110 MW sets. The total area of the factory and the township is around 2,650 acres. Construcion of the plant was started in 1963 and production was started in 1965.Even while the manufacture of products initially envisaged was being stabilised, there were indications from Planning Commission that the future additions to the country's power grid would be in the range of 200 and 500 MW sets and that, as such, the demand for 60 and 110 MW sets would taper off in coming years. This set in motion a series of diversification programmes. A number of new products were introduced at the Hyderabad Plant between 1971 and 1978 which included turbogenerator sets for captive power plants upto 60 MW, Centrifugal compressors, High speed Turbines, Pumps and Heat Exchangers for 210 MW power plants, boiler feed pump motors, Synchronous condensers, oil rigs, Bowl Mills, Turbo generator sets for captive power plants for steel and alluminium industries etc. The diversification was mostly in the industrial sector reducing the dependence of the unit on power sector. At present, the Hyderabad unit serves not only the power sector but also a wide range of industries viz., fertilizer, pertrochemicals, refineries, oil exploration, steel, aluminium, cement, sugar, chemicals, coal, railways etc. Because of the diversification measures, the unit could not only optimally utilise its capacity, but also record an impressive

1. *Ibid.*
2. BHEL, Annual Report, 1989-90.
3. *Ibid.*
4. *Ibid.*
5. BHEL, Personnel Manual, July, 1985, p. 1.1.3.

growth. The high quality of workmanship of BHEL, the Hyderabad unit, has earned recognition from International associations such as the American Society of Mechanical engineers, American Petroleum Institute etc.[1]

Table 2.1 shows the position of capital and employment in the Hyderabad unit of BHEL during the period 1982-83 to 1988-89. It is clear from this table that the amount of capital increased from Rs. 1254.30 to Rs. 1702.30 million during 1982-83 to 1988-89 and the number of employees increased marginally from 10,214 to 10,595 during the period.

Table 2.1 : Progress of BHEL in Terms of Capital and Employment

Year	*Capital (Rs. in Millions)*	*Employment*
1982–83	1,254.30	10,214
1983–84	1,366.00	10,535
1984–85	1,433.50	10,531
1985–86	1,436.50	10,607
1986–87	1,535.67	10,617
1987–88	1,638.70	10,596
1988–89	1,702.30	10,592

Source : Growth Profile, B.H.E.L., Hyderabad,

The financial position of BHEL is presented in Table 2.2. It is clear from this table that the turnover of the BHEL went up by five times from Rs. 1831.90 millions to Rs. 4403 millions during 1982-83 to 1988-89 and profit rose up from Rs. 167.90 million to Rs. 340 millions during the period.

The position of industrial relations in terms of nimber of strikes, lockouts and mandays lost due to strikes and lockouts in BHEL during the period 1982-83 to 1988-89 is presented in Table 2.3. It is surprising to observe that there were no strikes and lockouts and no mandays were lost during the period. It is a sign of sound industrial relations.

The Hyderabad unit of BHEL has a number of diversification programmes on hand. With a nimber of discoveries of gas in the oil and the Government's decision to allocate gas for power generation, the Hyderabad unit has started manaufacturing gas turbines. Also manufac-

1. Tallur, N.S. *op.cit.*, p. 2.

Table 2.2 : Financial Position of BHEL during 1982–83 and 1988–89

(Rs. in millions)

Year	*Turnover*	*Profit*
1982–83	1,831.90	167.90
1983–84	2,392.10	100.94
1984–85	3,096.40	109.90
1985–86	3,692.70	355.80
1986–87	N.A.	N.A.
1987–88	3,892.90	460.00
1988–89	4,403.00	340.00

Source : Annual Reports and Growth Profile, B.H.E.L., Hyderabad.

N.A.: Not Available

Table 2.3 : Position of Industrial Relations in BHEL during 1982–83 and 1988–89

Year	*No. of Strikes*	*No. of Lockouts*	*Mandays lost*
1982–83	Nil	Nil	Nil
1983–84	Nil	Nil	Nil
1984–85	Nil	Nil	Nil
1985–86	Nil	Nil	Nil
1986–87	Nil	Nil	Nil
1987–88	Nil	Nil	Nil
1988–89	Nil	Nil	Nil

Source : BHEL Personnel Manual.

ture of new types of rigs for oil exploration industry viz., desert rigs, mobile rigs and work over rigs is being stabilised. In order to cater to the requirements of power plants which have to work in low grade coal of high ash content, the Hyderabad unit has also started manufacturing ball mills (for pulvarisation of coal). In addition, widening the manufacturing base, Hyderabad unit has been developed into a centre for offering turn key services for thermo-mechanical systems viz., co-generation plants, combined cycle plants, waster heat recovery systems etc. The Hyderabad unit has already completed two major projects for Bharat Petroleum Corporation Ltd. (BPCL) and Oil and Natural Gas Commission (ONGC).[1]

Future plans of Hyderabad plant include taking up of the manufacture of equipment for the Defence Sector, large scale desalination plants, gas insulted switch gear, pumps and heat exchangers for petrochemical plants etc. In the area of services renovation of old power plants and oil rigs, contract drilling etc., are being contemplated.[2]

(b) Profile And Progress of TISCO

Steel which provides the frame work of modern civilization, is the most versatile of all materials so far known to man. The development of modern urban civilization, agriculture equipments, war products, and a host of consumer durables are possibe because of the intelligent utilisation of iron and steel. Manufacture of iron and steel is considered the basic need to a nation's economic life. The production and consumption of iron and steel is rightly considered a sine-qua-non of country's industrial prosperity.

Development of industries including Iron and Steel was late in India, compared to the West. But India is considered to be the first producer of carbon steel (Wootz) which was highly priced in the world market.[3] The process of smelting iron ore in different types of furnaces disappeared during the nineteenth centrury after the establishment of British rule in India and the incidence of technological advance in Europe.[4]

The Tata Iron and Steel Company (TISCO), India's first integrated steel plant, was established under private sector in Jamshedpur, Bihar, in 1912. It remained the only integrated steel plant in India till the end of the fifties. As a result of the Government's policy of establishing capital intensive industries after independence, the first blast furnace of Rourkela Steel Plant was commissioned in 1959. The works of Bhilai Steel Plant was inaugurated in 1959; first production of Iron in Durgapur commenced in 1959; and Bokaro Steel was promoted in 1964 all being in public sectors.

---

1. *Ibid.*
2. *Ibid.*
3. Chaudhuri, M.R. "*Iron and Steel Industry of India, An Economic, Geographic appraisal,*" Oxford and IBH Publishing Company, Calcutta, 1975, p. 22.
4. Johnson, William, A., "*The Steel Industry of India,*" Oxford University Press, Bombay, 1967, p. 8.

TISCO acquires its raw materials from its captive mines and collieries in Bihar and Orissa. Beginning with 0.093 million tonnes of Steel in 1915-16 the Steel production raised to 0.500 million tonnes in 1924 under the greater extension programme. This phase saw the introduction of the Duplex process in the company. A third Duplex furnance was added in 1929, two new roughing and finishing mills (in 1933) and a new blast furnance (in 1935) were also added. With the addition of these installations, the plant's capacity reached 0.800 million tonnes of saleable steel by 1939.

The main products of TISCO are Semis, Bars, Rounds, Seamless bars, Structurals, Beams, Channels, Track materials, Tyres, Plates, Hot rolled sheets, Hot rolled strips, Forged products and other special products.

The annual crude steel capacity of TISCO at the end of Phase-II is expected to increase to 2.5 million tonnes and saleable steel to 2.1 million tonnes. Modernisation Phase-II will be followed by Phase-III inwhich the thrust will be on economies of scale, higher productivity, better quality and energy conservation.

The introduction of new technology in TISCO has been a process which has always been planned well inadvance for its smoothe execution. The bringing in of new technology has helped the mangement in a big way. It is percieved that the emphasis on choosing new technology has, by and large, been on the consideration of "returns on investment", which has led to higher production, productivity and profitability of the company. It has also, no doubt, led to better earnings of employees through incentives and annual bonus schemes.

Beginning with an output of 0.093 million tonnes of saleable steel in 1915-16, the company produced 2.314 million tonnes of crude steel and 1.944 million tonnes of finished steel in the year 1988-89.[1] This was possible largely due to an all time high production of liquid iron which stood at 2.239 million tonnes in the year 1988-89. The company has been operating above its installed capacity and registered a record performance for the last eight year (i.e., 1980-89).[2]

The progress of TISCO in terms of capital and employment is presented in Table 2.4. It is clear from this table that capital increased

1. Tata Steel, Corporate Report, 1989.
2. Kast, F.E., and Rosenzwieg, J.E., "*Organisation and Management*," Mc Graw-Hill Publishing Company, New York, 1984, p. 198.

from Rs. 834.4 million to Rs. 1560.9 million whereas employment rose up from 69,723 to 89,000 during the period 1982-83 to 1988-89.

Table 2.5 shows that financial position of TISCO during the period 1982-89. It is clear from this Table that the sales turnover increased narly two times whereas profit recorded four-fold increase during the period.

Industrial relations position in terms of number of strikes, lockouts and mandays lost are shown in Table 2.6. It is evident from this table that there were no strikes, lockouts and mandays lost. It indicates harmonious industrial relations in this organisation.

Table 2.4 : Progress of TISCO in Terms of Capital and Employment

Year	*Capital (Rs. in Millions)*	*Employment*
1982–83	834.40	69,723
1983–84	720.20	70,011
1984–85	720.20	70,567
1985–86	827.40	71,100
1986–87	826.30	76,187
1987–88	1,360.10	82,736
1988–89	4,560.90	89,000

Source : TISCO Annual Reports

Table 2.5 : Financial Position of TISCO during 1982–83 and 1988–89

(*Rs. in millions*)

Year	*Turnover*	*Profit*
1982–83	7,981.60	448.70
1983–84	8,895.40	200.10
1984–85	11,050.20	967.40
1985–86	12,855.10	1,576.80
1986–87	14,163.90	995.20
1987–88	15,267.80	1,121.50
1988–89	18,617.70	1,803.40

Source : TISCO Annual Reports

Table 2.6 : Position of Industrial Relations in TISCO during 1982–83 and 1988–89

Year	*No. of Strikes*	*No. of Lockouts*	*Mandays lost*
1982–83	Nil	Nil	Nil
1983–84	Nil	Nil	Nil
1984–85	Nil	Nil	Nil
1985–86	Nil	Nil	Nil
1986–87	Nil	Nil	Nil
1987–88	Nil	Nil	Nil
1988–89	Nil	Nil	Nil

Source : TISCO, Concept of working together.

2. Organisation Structure of BHEL and TISCO

Organisation structure is the established pattern of relationships among the component parts of the organisation.[1] The structure of organisation is an essential means for achieving the organisational goals.

The top mangement team of TISCO comprises the Chairman and Managing Director, Deputy Chairman, Vice-chairman, Joint-Managing Director, Executive Director (Operations), Executive Director (Industrial Relations), Executive Director (Corporate), Executive Director (Raw Materials).

They are supported by a team of experts, except the Deputy Chairman and Vice-Chairman, all the others are full-time employees of the company. The persons directly report to the Chairman and Managing Director CMD), *viz.*, the Joint Managing Director, and the Executive Director Corporate. The personnel cell also reports to the CMD, through the Director (Personnel).

The functional heads of finance, accounts, marketing, public relations and export functions report to the Executive Director (corporate). All other functional heads report to the Joint Managing Director through Executive Director.

The Executive Director (operations) looks after the functions of works, central engineering and development division, scientific services, commercial, personnel and establishment. The Executive Director-

1. *Ibid.*

Industrial Relation looks after the industrial relation matters of all the divisions of Tata Steel and its subsidiaries. The Executive Director (Raw materials) looks after the mines and collieries. The General Manager (Works) is assisted by Assistant General managers of various divisions.

Each group consists of several works departments, categorised on the basis of functions/services they render, and headed by a superintendent, Additional Superintendents and Assistant Superintendents.

One Personnel Officer/Senior Personnel Officer is incharge of personnel function of one large department each of a group of 2-3 small departments. They report to the assistant chief personnel managers, who in turn report to the Deputy Director (Personnel) concerned. The functions of industrial relations are different from personnel at Tata Steel.

The board of Trustees is the highest body in BHEL Corporate Sector. The Chairman and Managing director is the head of the organisation followed by mangement committee. The BHEL organisation is divided into three sectors viz., corporate functions, business sectors, and operating units.

Corporate functions consist of all the functional departments headed by the directors. Business sector consists of various activities of the organisation which are headed by full-time directors.

There are different operating units which are located at various parts of the country, each manged by an executive Director.

The Hyderabad unit of BHEL's organisation is headed by a full time executive Director. The organisaion is divided into two groups *viz.*, (1) Product groups and (2) Services and functions. The Departmentalisation has been done on the basis of the product. There ar six departments in the product group. There are seven departments in the services and functions. Each Department is headed by a General Manager and each department is again divided on the basis of functions, and each division is headed by a Deputy General Manager. The Deputy General manager is assisted by Senior Manager, Manger, Deputy Manger etc.

Review of Literature

Though public and private sectors are growing very rapidly in India, comparative studies dealing with participative mangement and quality circles in public and private sector industries are very limited. However, there are a few Government reports and research studies. The

Ministry of Labour and employment[1] has studied the working of the Joint Management Councils in 30 units based on various factors like industrial relations, stability of work force, accidents, production and productivity etc. It was recommended in that report that more stress be laid on workers' education, involvement of the middle management personnel and still more on the sharing of information. Another report of the Ministry of Labour and Employment which studied Joint Management Councils[2] in 99 industries (65 in private and 34 in public), indicated the limited success of these councils in India.

Among other studies, Das's[3] study points out the lack of interest on the part of the labour and management in the scheme originating from mutual suspicious atmosphere that characterised industrial relations scheme in India.

Kennedy[4], Subramanian[5], Tanic[6], Kannappan[7] and Virmani[8] have reviewed the overall working of the councils at the macro level. These studies have shown that the failure of the councils is due to the prevailing industrial relations and indicated that effective collective bargaining is a pre–requisite for the success of any scheme of joint consultation.

Pandit[9] studied the working of the JMCs in four private sector units. Her analysis was based on the functions of the JMCs, their performance,

1. Government of India, Ministry of Labour and Employment, "*Reports on the Working of the Joint Management councils*" The Author, New Delhi, 1965.
2. Ministry of Labour and Employment, Government of India, "*Reports on the Working of the Joint Management Councils,*" The Author, New Delhi, 1966.
3. Das, Nabagopal, *op. cit.*
4. Kennedy, Van D., "*Unions, Employers and Government : Essays on Indian Labour Questions*", Manaktala and Sons, Bombay, 1966.
5. Subramanian, K. N., "*Labour Management Relations in India*", Asia Publishing House, Bombay, 1967.
6. Tanic Zivan, "*Workers' participation in Management : Ideal and Reality in India*", Shri Ram Centre for Industrial Relations and Human Resources, New Delhi, 1969.
7. Kannappan, Subbaiah, "*Workers' Participation in Management : A Review of Indian Experience*", Bulletin of International Institute of Labour Studies, No. 5, November, 1968.
8. Virmani, B.R., *op. cit.*
9. Pandit, D.P., "*Workers' Participation in Management : The Indian experiments*", Mimeograph Report submitted to the Institute of Economic Growth, New Delhi, 1962.

the nature of decisions taken in them, the context of co–operation between the parties etc. She observed that the size, structure, decision–making etc., were irrelavant as long as the groups involved in the councils lack the spirit of co–operation. The workers' involvement and participation is higher when their representation is based on election.

Mehtras[1] studied JMCs in five units taking into account their evolution, structure, functions and results, The evaluation of the councils was based on their impact on production and productivity, labour welfare, absenteeism, accidents and the overall industrial relations situation. The findings of the study reval that the council had a negligible impact on the above factors.

Sheth[2] in his study examined the determinants of the attitudes, strengths and weaknesses based on the working of the participative management scheme in six units. He observed that JMCs introduced voluntarily worked somewhat (in terms of frequency of meetings and attitudes of the parties) better than those introduced on the basis of the tripartite recommendations.

Alexander[3] studied the working of participative management in two textile mills with a sample of 102 respondents. He analysed the working of bipartite forums in terms of their institutionalization, memebrs' attendance at the meetings, meetings held etc. He concluded that institutionalization of participative management might lead to better organisational health and effectiveness, and particpative management was better institutionalized in an organization where the management was genuinly interested in the process of participative management.

Aziz[4] has conducted his study based on eight factors. His study aimed at evaluating the degree of power and authority that the employers have shared with labour under the scheme and assessing the return flow of power and authority to management viewed in terms of control acquired in regard to discipline at work place, worker efficiency, absenteeism and industrial relations. The important finding of the study

1. Mehtras, V.G., op. cit.
2. Sheth, N. R. op. cit.
3. Alexander, K. C., "Participative Management : The Indian Experience", Shri Ram Centre for Industrial Relations and Human Resources, New Delhi, 1972.
4. Aziz, Abdul, "*Workers' Participation in Management : Indian Experiences*", Ashish Publishing House, New Delhi, 1980.

is that all types of respondents have preferred to participate at shop than at board level.

Laxmi Narain[1] has conducted a macro level study in 40 public enterprises to study the attitudes and approaches of managers and trade union members on participation and a detailed micro–level study of the working of the participative forums in a large public enterprise. The significant finding of the macro–level study is that all the parties have much faith in the potentiality and promise of the scheme of workers' participation in management. That top management has no interest in the proceedings of the participative management is the major finding in the micro–level study conducted by him.

Pylee[2] conducted three different studies on participative management. The findings are also different. His first study on a private Electronics company revealed that the workers do not have faith in the scheme. The finding of the second study on a public sector Aluminium Industry, is that both the workers and management have belief in the participative councils and also a high sense of belonging. His third study on hospital management indicated that the participative management scheme is successful as it provided necessary satisfaction for the employees.

Pramanil[3] examined that attitudes of workers and management towards participative management in eight public sector units. His findigs are that the management attitude towards workers is often legalistic and that many of them are still unable to recognise the right of the workers to organize. The management felt that the trade union is acting as their rival organization.

Varandani[4] conducted his study on the operation of the scheme of Joint Management Council in selected industries and on making workers shareholders in India.

Sahu[5] in his study covered five public and five private sector

1. Laxmi Narain, "*Workers' Participation in Public Enterprises*", Himalaya Publishing House, Bombay, 1984.
2. Pylee, M. V. *op. cit.*
3. Pramil, S. "*Personnel Management and Productivity in Public Secotr Industries in India*", Unpublished Ph.D., Thesis, Bhurdwan University, 1975.
4. Varandani, Gurusharan, *op. cit.*
5. Sahu, Bhabatosh, "*Dynamics of Participative Management : Indian Experiences*", Himalaya Publishing House, Bombay, 1970.

industries, and he made a special study of two steel plants, one in public and another in private sector. His study covered the results of participative management and the opinions of the participants on the working of the scheme. The level of satisfaction relating to the participative management scheme was covered in this study.

Gopal[1] studied the working of the scheme of participative management in one of the units of the Indian Railways i.e., Diesel Locomotive Works, Varanasi. The study has been made in detail relating to the evaluation of the organizational structure, factors influencing the functioning of the scheme, and the attitude of the management and workers towards the scheme.

Rath[2] has conducted his study on the working and impact of participative management in Rourkela Steel Plant. He studied the ways that the scheme of participative management is institutionalised, the working of the schemes in terms of frequency of meetings held, recommendations passed and recommendations implemented by the management and the impact of participative management. He concluded that the experience of participative management in Rourkela Steel Plant is a reality dispelling the misnomer of myth.

Ramesh and Narasimha Rao[3] studied the participative management in Visakhapatnam Port Trust. Their study covered the levels suitable to the effective performance of the participative management, evaluated the working of the participative management in terms of objectives and identified the gaps between the objectives and practice relating to the scheme of participative management.

Pandy[4], in his study on Human Resources Management in TISCO, covered selection, recruitment, personnel policies, collective bargaining, industrial relations situation, communication, grievance procedure, participative management etc., in TISCO. Participative management was covered in only one chapter in his study.

1. Gopal, Vishnu, "*Industrial Democracy in India*", Chugh Publications, Allahabad, 1984.
2. Bhabani Prasad Rath, *op. cit.*
3. Ramesh, K. and Narasimha Rao, GB VL, "*Participative Management*", Ajanta Publications (India), New Delhi, 1990.
4. Pandey, S. N. "*Human Side of Tata Steel*", Tata McGraw–Hill Publishing House, New Delhi. 1989

Review of Literature on Quality Circles

The concept of quality circles is of recent origin and it is in an experimental stage in India. Hence, much research has not been done in India. However, a few research papers on the working of the quality circles have been published. The Central Labour Institute[1] has conducted a study on how quality circle programmes were being launched and implemented and to what extent the concept has been accepted. The study states that the quality circles were launched and implemented systematically at BHEL.

There are no further studies on workers' participation in management and quality circles in TISCO. The same is the case with BHEL. And there is no study on comparitive analysis of public and private sector industrial units. While some of the studies placed greater emphasis on macro level analysis, other studies limited their scope to particular form of participative scheme and quality circles. Consequently the working of participative management was not studied at the micro level in the vital public and private sector industrial units in the country viz., BHEL and TISCO.

Hence, it is felt that there is a greater need for a competitive study of workers' participation in the management and quality circles in the vital public and private secotr industrial units in the country.

Objectives, Methodology and Sampling.

The present study is designed and carried out with the following objectives.

1. To examine the structure of participative forums in the unit under study;
2. to enquire into the working of participative forums;
3. to evaluate the impact of participative management schemes, on selected variables; and
4. to study the working of Quality Circles and their impact on selected variables.

In order to attain the objectives stated above, information was collected from both the primary and the secondary sources. Primary data was collected through a schedule administered among the sample respon-

---

1. Central Labour Institute, "*Tangible gains of Quality Circles*"' Study published in S.R. Udpa, Quality Circles in India, Tata McGraw–Hill Publication, New Delhi, 1986.

dent participants with a view to making the study more objective and meaningful. Informal discussions with the management and union leaders were carried out, with a view to soliciting their rich experiences.

In addition to the primary data collected, secondary sources of information were also relied upon, to the extent needed. Secondary data was obtained from the records of the two organizations *viz.*, annual reports, minutes of participative councils, personnel manual, in–house journals etc.

Sampling

The number of members representing the participative forums at three levels in the two organizations is presented in Table 2.7. It is observed from the table that the number of management and worker representative are equal at each level in both the organisations.

It is decided to select at least one leader/deputy leader and one ordinary member from each category of respondents from each council. This gives a minimum of two respondents of each category and a total of four respondents from each council. The same ratio is maintained in selecting sample at all levels. It is decided to select the sample at the rate of 25.00 per cent of the population (the total number of members at all levels are 248 in BHEL and 742 in TISCO, the total being 990) based on the stratified random sample technique by following the above mentioned criteria. The sample is kept around 25 per cent to the maximum possible extent. The number of management and workers representatives are nine each at the apex level council in BHEL. A sample of two respondents each of management representatives and worker representatives is selected. There are 11 members each at the apex council in TISCO. A sample of two each at the management and worker representatives is selected basing on the basis of the above mentioned criteria. There are two councils at the plant level and 22 members each of management and worker representatives in BHEL. A sample of four members each of the management and worker representatives is selected. There is only one plant council and 13 members each of management and workers representatives in TISCO. A sample of two representatives each of management and workers is selected.

There are 12 shop councils and 93 members each at the lower level in BHEL. A sample of 24 members each of management and worker representatives is selected in BHEL. There are 47 shop councils and 347 members each management and worker representatives at the lower level

Table 2.7 : Members Representing the Participative Forums and Sample Selected

Level of Council	BHEL							TISCO							Total		
	No. of Councils	Population			Sample			No. of Councils	Population			Sample			Sample		
		MR	WR	T	MR	WR	T		MR	WR	T	MR	WR	T	MR	WR	T
Grass–Root	12	93	93	186	24	24	48	47	347	347	694	94	94	188	118	118	236
Middle level	2	22	22	44	4	4	8	1	13	13	26	2	2	4	6	6	12
Apex level	1	9	9	18	2	2	4	1	11	11	22	2	2	4	4	4	8
Total	**15**	**124**	**124**	**248**	**30**	**30**	**60**	**49**	**371**	**371**	**742**	**98**	**98**	**196**	**128**	**128**	**256**

MR—Management Representatives WR—Worker Representatives T—Total

in TISCO. A sample of 94 members each of management and worker representatives is selected basing on the above mentioned criteria.

There are 352 quality circles functioning in 30 functional areas in BHEL in different departments. Similarly, there are only 12 quality circles in 10 major functional areas in TISCO. A sample of 10 per cent of the total quality circles is selected on the basis of stratified random sampling techniques representing atleast one from each major functional area. Thus, 35 quality circles representing all the major functional areas are selected in BHEL. Ten quality circles one from each of the functional areas are selected from TISCO. The percentage of the sample is more than 10.00 per cent in case of TISCO as there are only 10 circles in ten areas.

Presentation of the Study

The study is presented in Six Chapters—

Chapter–I outlines the need for harmonious relations, the industrial relations scene in India and the role of participative management in promoting harmonious relations, it also deals with the origin and growth of participative schemes of workers' participation in public and private sectors, the quality circles and growth of the quality circles in India.

Chapter–II outlines the objectives, methodology, sampling and the industrial units under study.

The structure and working of the participative management at different levels i.e., grass root, middle and apex level are presented in *Chapter–III*.

Chapter–IV measures the impact of participative management on the organizations' production and productivity, working conditions, welfare etc.

Chapter–V reviews the working and impact of quality circles in the organizations, and

Chapter–VI evaluates the major findings and suggests steps for effective and successful functioning of participative management and quality circles.

Limitations

The study has been confined to two units and it is not free from limitations. A major difficulty the researcher faced was the non–availability of organized and upto–date data in some areas. It was very difficult to administer the questionaire on management and workers. The managers were busy in their work schedules and other activities. Some of the workers did not agree to respond to the questionnaire. Though the members agreed to respond to the questionnaire their responses were indifferent.

The size of the both the organization being huge the researcher faced great difficulties in the task of administering the questionnaires on the workers and managers.

3

Structure and Working of Participative Management

Origin and Growth of Participative Management Schemes in BHEL and TISCO

1. BHEL

Participative management scheme was introduced in BHEL in the form of National Bi–partite Joint Committee in 1973. This committee is popularly known as Joint Committee at apex level. The National Bi–partite Joint Committee consist of the representatives of management and employees drawn from the local unions and the national trade union centres. Within a short span of less than three years the bi–partite forum at the apex had to its credit a number of outstanding achievements including formulation of welfare policies, rationalization of job nomenclature and lines of progression and evolution of rational incentive payment system applicable uniformly to all the plants under the company[1]. Consistently throughout its tenure, the effort of the joint committees has been directed towards consolidating the climate of industrial harmony and co–operation providing better life to the employees through increase production and productivity. No single man–hour was lost during the period 1973–75 on account of industrial strife. That the atmosphere of cordiality was accompanied by significant achievements in the production front is an eloquent testimony to the effectiveness and

1. BHEL, "*Power to the People*", Corporate Personnel Division, 1976.

success of the participative endeavour in the joint committee.

Inspired by the achievements of participation at the apex level, the BHEL has extended the scope of joint committees to new operational areas such as optimization of production, development of skills and provisions of training facilities, management of physical environment at work place etc. The management realized that the need has arisen for extending participation and involvement that characterize the participative endeavour at the apex permeating down to the grass-root level[1]. Keeping the above points and the directive of Government of India regarding the institution of the participative management schemes at the middle and grass-root level in view the management and employee representatives of BHEL, after mutual discussion and agreement, evolved a scheme of workers' participation in management in 1975, designed to use them into the heart of production process and to give them a reasonable share of control and authority over their work and their place[2]. This scheme of workers' participation in management consists of joint councils (i.e., at middle level) and shop council (i.e., at grass-root level). Thus, workers' participation in management functions at three levels in BHEL viz., Joint Committee at apex level, Joint councils at middle level and shop councils at grass-root level.

2. TISCO

The scheme of closer association of employees with management is a major step towards the establishment of industrial democracy in Tata Iron and Steel Company Limited (TISCO). TISCO reached this milestone after passing through the stage of "deputation", "consultation" and "association". The first joint works committee in the company was constituted in 1919. Due to various reasons, the experiment did not meet with success and therefore, discontinued. It was revived again in 1946 with the formation of the West Plant Joint Committee and East Plant Joint Committee for departments in the Western and Eastern zones of the works respectively and the ministerial staff joint committee for the office staff, with the coming into effect of the Industrial Disputes Act of 1947. These committees were again reconstituted in 1948. During the decade 1946–56, altogether 24 Joint Committees were formed to deal with grievances, rates, minimum qualifications and employees services. But more important from the point of view of employees was their association with the

1. *Ibid.*
2. *Ibid.*

operational performance of the production department committees, having equal number of representatives from both the management and the union. These committees discussed all problems having a bearing on production and recommended suitable corrective measures to management[1].

The organization can legitimately take credit for working towards the objective of setting joint councils before government made the recommendation for the firm action of such councils. In 1952, a British expert, who was commissioned to advise the company on management matters, suggested the setting up of a joint consultative machinery. Three years later, a top official of the company was sent to West Germany to attend an international conference on joint consultation and later to study the various pattern of employee association with management in a number of European countries, such as West Germany, Belgium, Sweden and Yugoslavia. On the basis of his report and after intensive study of all the aspects of the matter, the company was well set to formulate its plan for a machinery for Closer Association of employees with management, in keeping with its traditions and suited to its needs[2]. The present scheme of Closer Association of employees with management was the result of the two agreements between the management and the union in the year 1956. The main objectives of the Closer Association are—

i) to promote increased productivity for the general benefit of the enterprises, the employees, and the country
ii) to give employees a better understanding of their role and importance in the working of the industry and in the process of production, and
iii) satisfy the urge for self–expression.

Structure of the Participative Management

1. Organization of Participative Management

An important determinant of the successful sharing of power between management and labour is the building of the right type of organization structure. "Organization structure simply refers to the nature of inter–relationships established between the different groups of indi-

1. Sahu, Bhabatosh, "*Participative Management for Effective Human Resources Management; Experience of two Steel Plants*". in Kholi and Goutam (Eds.) "Human Resources Development and the Planning Process in India" Vikas Publishing House Pvt. Ltd., New Delhi, 1988, p. 182.

1. *Ibid.*, p. 183.

viduals who are engaged in attaining the organizational goals[1]". Participative management is also an organ of the organization structure of an industry. According to Miller and Form, "joint consultation machinery may be explained as a formal organization of employees and management representatives who exchange information and advice and in some cases make decisions on matters of common concern[2]".

The structure of participative management in both the organizations is a three–tier set up. The present scheme in TISCO was initiated in the year 1956 as a voluntary measure whereas in BHEL the present set up was originally started at apex level in 1973 and extended to middle level and grass–root level in 1975.

The structure of participative management in BHEL comprises of 12 hop Councils (at grass–root level), two Joint Councils at plant level and one Joint Committee at apex level[3]. Each shop council was set up for one or more shops or departments in the plant depending upon the number of employees in different shops/departments. The plant council is set up for each plant of the country. The two plant councils have come into existence, one for Heavy Power Equipment Plant (HPEP) and one for Switch Gear in Ramachandrapuram unit of BHEL. The tenure of shop and plant councils is two years. There is one joint committee at apex level of the BHEL. There are 47 Joint Departmental Councils (JDCs) at grass–root level, one Joint Works Council (JWC) at middle level and one Joint Consultative Council of Management (JCCM) at apex level in TISCO[4]. The tenure of each council is two years. It is clear from the above that workers' participation in management is not extended to the level of Board of Directors—policy making body of the organization. As such participative management bodies at apex level in both the organizations can only offer recommendations to Board of Directors but not make decisions. Hence, it is suggested that the managements of both the organizations should convert the schemes of participative management at apex level in the present scheme as participation at Board of Directors level as proposed in Workers' participation in Management Bill, 1990[5].

1. Aziz, Abdul, *op. cit.*, p. 45.
2. Miller, D. C., and Form, W.H., "*Industrial Sociology : The Sociology of Work Organization*", Harper & Row Publishers, New York, 1964, p. 758.
3. BHEL Personnel Manual, *op. cit.*, p. 6.6.2.
4. Tata Steel, Constitution of Joint Committee of Joint Consultations, p. 12.
5. Badruddin, "*Management, workers' participation and the law*", Deep and Deep Publications, New Delhi, 1991, pp. 130–140.

The schemes of participative management in both the organizations have the authority to make recommendations on various issues to the management. Management makes decisions considering these recommendations. But, this nature may lead to non–consideration of the recommendations of the various forums of participative management and hence functioning of participative management may be formality rather than a necessity. Hence, it is suggested that the management of BHEL and TISCO should delegate the authority of decisions making to various participative management councils.

Each council in both the organizations is administered by a Chairman, a Vice–Chairman, and a Secretary. Each council in TISCO constitutes a small agenda sub–committee with an equal number of representatives of management and the employees. The representatives of this committee are elected from among the members of the councils. The main function of the sub–committee is to prepare the agenda of council meetings. It does not rely on its own resources exclusively, and contacts employees in the different sections of the department for this purpose. In the case of BHEL, the secretary of the council concerned prepares the agenda in consultation with the members. It would be difficult to secretary alone to contact the members, collect the issues and prepare the agenda. Further, it many give rise to suspicious to the members that the agenda is not prepared in good faith. Hence, it is suggested that the management and trade unions at BHEL should restructure their organization of participative management by incorporating agenda sub–committee in all the councils at all levels.

2. Objectives and Functions of Participative Management in BHEL and TISCO

The main objectives of the participative management councils in BHEL are (i) to improve production (ii) to provide better safety and welfare facilities and working conditions, (iii) to satisfy the employees regarding wages and the need for self–expression[1].

The objectives of council at various levels in TISCO[2] are to associate, in an increasing measure, workers/employees with management in the working of the industry with a view to :

a) promoting increased productivity for the general benefit of the enterprise, the employee and the country,

1. BHEL, Personnel Manual, op. cit., p. 6.6.4.
2. Tata Steel, Constitution of Joint Committees of Joint Consultations, p. 12.

b) giving employees a better understanding of their role and importance in the working of the industry and in the process of production; and

c) satisfy the urge for self–expression.

It is observed that the management and the trade unions of both the organizations could not consider the important objectives of participative management like democratization of work place, human growth and dignity of work. Hence, it is suggested that these should also be incorporated in the objectives of workers' participation in management in BHEL and TISCO.

The functions of the shop councils[1] in BHEL include :

a) Fixation of production programmes and targets, productivity issues such as raw materials planning, work allocation, job redesign, job training etc.

b) Improvement of production, productivity and efficiency including elimination of wastage and optimum utilization of machine capacity and manpower.

c) Identification of specific areas responsible for low productivity and suggestion of necessary corrective steps at shop level.

d) Identification of reasons for absenteeism in the shops/departments and suggestion of remedial measures for its minimization.

e) Assistance in the maintenance and improvement of general discipline in the shop/department.

f) Making suggestions on the safety measures in the shop/department/plant.

g) Offering advice regarding the physical environment and working conditions.

h) Any other matter referred to it by the plant council for the consideration of shop council.

The functions of the joint council in BHEL include discussion, decision and solving the :

a) Problems emanating from shop councils which remain unsolved.

b) Matters concerning the unit or plant as a whole in respect of issue in connection with work process, work organization, work planning, work load, and manning.

1. BHEL, "*Personnel Manual*", *op. cit.*, p. 6.65.

c) Problems affecting more than one department/shop.
d) Issues of skills and abilities of employees.
e) Issue concerning the general health, welfare and safety measures relating to the plant as a whole.
f) Payment and rewards for valuable suggestions from employees.
g) Any matter referred to by the Joint Committee for consideration of the plant council.

The functions of the Joint Committee (Apex level) in BHEL include[1] discussion, decisions and solving the—

a) Issues relating to pay structure and revision.
b) Issues regarding fringe benefits, bonus, incentive payments, rationalization of leave facilities etc.
c) Issues concerning the production and productivity unsolved.

The functions of Joint Departmental Councils in TISCO[2] includes

a) studying operational results and current and long–term departmental productions problems.
b) advising on steps necessary at departmental level to promote and rationalize production; improvements, lay–out and processes; improve productivity and discipline; eliminate wastage, effect economies with a view to lowering costs, eliminate defective work and improve the quality of products; improve the upkeep and care of machinery, tools and instruments; promote efficient use of safety precautions and devices; promote employees welfare and activities like sports/picnics; encourage suggestions; improve working conditions and better functioning of the department;
c) implementing the recommendations or decisions of the joint consultative council of management or the joint works council approved by management.
d) referring, where necessary, any matter to the joint works council for their consideration or advice.

The functions of the Joint Works Council[3] in TISCO are :

a) to study operational results and current and long–term production problems of the works as a whole.

---

1. *Ibid.*, p. 6.6.6.
2. Tata Steel, constitution of Joint Committees for Joint Consultations, p. 12.
3. *Ibid.*

b) to advise on the steps necessary to promote and rationalize production; improve methods, layout and processes; improve productivity and discipline, eliminate waste; effect economies with a view to lowering costs; eliminate defective work and improve the quality of products; improve the upkeep and care of machinery, tools and instruments; promote efficient safety precautions and devices; promote employees activities like picnics, sports etc.

c) to follow-up the implementation through the appropriate JDC of its recommendations or decisions approved by management.

d) to refer any matter to the Joint Consultative Council of Management for their consideration or advice.

e) to advise on any matter referred to it by the JDC or by the JCCM or by Management.

The functions of Joint Consultative Council of Management in TISCO are[1] :

a) to advise management on all matters concerning the working of the industry in the fields of production and welfare.

b) to advise management in regard to economic and financial matters placed by management before the council, provided that the council may discuss questions dealing with general, economic and financial matters concerning the affecting the relations of the economy with its shareholders or managerial staff or other matters of confidential nature.

c) to consider the advice on any matter referred to it by the JWC.

d) to follow up the implementation through the JWC.

It is observed that some of the important functions relating to democratization of work place and human growth are not included in the function of participative management of both the organizations. Hence, it is suggested that in addition to the above functions the management and trade unions of both the organizations should also incorporate the functions relating to the objectives such as democratization of work place, human growth and dignity of work in all councils at all levels.

3. Membership Composition

Both the management and employees have their representatives in participative management bodies at various levels. The parties should

1. *Ibid.*

take proper care in nominating/electing their representatives. Employees possessing the skill of discussion and decision–making with adequate experience and aptitude in management, and the interest in serving the management extraordinarily should be selected as representatives. There should be equal representation to both management and workers groups.

Shop Councils in BHEL

The joint council in BHEL would determine the constituencies for the shop councils depending on the number of employees in various departments, functions or areas. While deciding on the total number of shop councils in the plant, care is taken to see that one shop council would represent a group of 800 to 1000 employees[1]. This is necessary to the one hand to make the shop councils adequately representative, and, on the other, to avoid the proliferation of shop councils which might otherwise pose operational problems. Each shop council consists of not more than 12 representatives of the employees and an equal number of representatives of he management.

The representatives of the employees in the shop council are nominated by the participating unions on the basis of percentage of votes polled in the union elections. The criterion followed is that those unions who secure 25% to 35% votes can nominate one person, unions who secure 35% to 55% can nominate 2 persons, and the unions who secure more than 55% can nominate 3 persons in the shop councils[2]. For the purpose of the nomination of the representatives of the workers to the shop council, the shop/department is divided into a suitable number of constituencies and each union will nominate the prescribed number of representatives from each constituency.

The management group consists of members in the proportion of one member each from the Senior Management level (Senior Manager/ Manager), Middle Management level (Dy. Manager/Sr. Engineer) and Junior Management level (Engineers), and two from the supervisory group. The Head of the Department (Sr. Management level/Managerial level) is generally the Chairman of the council and he will also act as the secretary of the council. Management representatives are chosen by General Manager who may call for the advice and assistance of the personnel department and the Head of the Department concerned[3]. The Co–chairman for the shop council is nominated from among the em-

1. BHEL, Personnel Manual, p. 6.6.3.
2. *Ibid.*
3. *Ibid.*

ployee representatives in the shop council. Unions will be impressed upon the need to nominate their representatives from among those who are considered to be good in terms of output, attendance and discipline and who enjoy general acceptance of the employees in the shop. There should be a proper ratio of representation of all parties concerned as members in participative management scheme in order to have required weightage. Generally, it is agreed that the management and employees represent equality in participative management schemes.

Joint Councils in BHEL

Joint council consists of a maximum of 12 members each from management and workers. The procedure of nominating the worker representatives is the same as followed in shop councils. The Management representatives consists of General Manager, who also acts as the Chairman of the council, Heads of the Departments of production, personnel, finance, engineering and materials, two from executives, two from amongst the supervisors, and two from amongst the Chairman of the shop councils. The co–Chairman of the Council is nominated from among workers.

Joint Committee in BHEL

For the Joint Committee at apex level also, the workers are nominated following the same procedure. Besides these workers, the members from central trade unions will also be nominated. The management representatives consists of Chairman and Managing Director, functional directors and Heads of the Divisions. The Chairman and Managing Director acts as the Chairman of the Joint Committee and the Co–Chairman is nominated from among workers representatives.

It is observed from the Table 2.7 that there is equal representation of both the management and employees in all the councils.

The tenure of the shop and joint councils is two years, whereas the tenure of the apex level council is decided by the Committee itself. But normally the tenure is two years.

TISCO

The JDCs, depending on the size of the department/departments, consists of two to ten representatives of management and an equal number of representatives of workers/employees, including a fair representation from the supervisory units of the Tata Workers' Union (TWU). The representatives of the management are nominated by the management and those of employees are nominated by the Union from among employees of the company. The management is planning to introduce gradually the principle of election by secret ballot in the selection of employee representatives[1]. The Joint works council consists of 13 representatives of the management and an equal number of representatives of employees. The representatives of management are nominated by the management. The representatives of the employees, including a fair representation of employees within the sphere of the supervisory unit of the union, will be nominated by the union from among the employees of the company. The Chairmanship and Vice–Chairmanship of the council is alternatively held by the management and union representative for a year each.

The Joint Consultative Council of Management (JCCM) consists of 11 representatives of management and an equal number of representatives of employees, including the Chairman and the Co–Chairman of the Council. The management representatives are nominated by the company. The worker representatives are nominated by the Union. The Chairmanship and Co–Chairmanship are by rotation between workers and management every year. It is observed from Table 2.7 that the number of representatives of both management and workers are equal in all the councils in the company.

It is observed that there are three important issues in the structure of various councils of the two organizations viz., (a) the basis of selection of the representatives, (b) the basis of nomination of the representatives, if nomination method of selection is preferred, and (c) the appointment of Chairman and Co–Chairman from among worker and management representatives.

a) Basis of Selection of the Representatives

There are two methods for selecting the representatives, viz., nomination method and election method. At present, the nomination method is followed by both management and trade unions in the two organizations. But the management of TISCO is contemplating to introduce the system of election to select the worker representatives. Further, some of the workers' representatives in BHEL also prefer the election method. Hence an attempt is made to solicit the preferences of the members regarding the basis of selection.

Table 3.1 shows the members' preference regarding the mode of

1. Tata Steel, Constitution of Joint Committees of Joint Consultations.

Table 3.1 : Members' Preference Regarding Mode of Selection

(Members responses are indicated in percentage)

Preference	BHEL						TISCO					
	Shop Council		*Joint Council*		*Joint Committee*		*Joint Departmental Council*		*Joint Works Council*		*Joint Consultative Council of Management*	
	M.R. N=24	W.R. N=24	M.R. N=4	W.R. N=4	M.R. N=2	W.R. N=2	M.R. N=94	W.R. N=94	M.R. N=2	W.R. N=2	M.R. N=2	W.R. N=2
Election	29.17	41.67	25.00	25.00	---	---	29.79	45.74	---	50.00	---	100.00
Nomination	70.83	58.33	75.00	75.00	100.00	100.00	70.21	54.26	100.00	50.00	100.00	---
Total	**100.00**	**100.00**	**100.00**	**100.00**	**100.00**	**100.00**	**100.00**	**100.00**	**100.00**	**100.00**	**100.00**	**100.00**

M.R. : Management Representatives; W.R. : Workers' Representatives

Source : Data is collected through questionnaire.

selection of members to the various schemes of participative management. It is observed from the table that a majority of the members (70.83 per cent of management and 58.33 per cent of workers' representatives at the shop council) of BHEL preferred nomination method. Similar opinion is observed from the members of TISCO's Joint departmental council. At the middle level, three–fourths of the management representatives and three–fourths of worker representatives of BHEL preferred the nomination method. In TISCO all the management representatives and half of the worker representatives at JWC preferred the nomination method. At the top level all the management representatives and nearly three–fourths of worker representatives from the both of organizations preferred nomination method.

Thus, the majority of the members of management and workers prefer the method of nomination in the selection of members to the councils, probably with a view to avoiding political activity, in case of elections. Hence, it is suggested that the management of TISCO should drop the idea of introducing the election system to select the workers' representatives and continue the present system of nomination.

b) Basis of Nomination of the Representatives

It is observed from the above analysis that the representatives of both the management and workers are appointed by nomination. There are no clear basis for nomination. Hence, the opinions of the members of participative councils about the criteria followed in nominating members to councils are collected and presented in Table 3.2. It is observed from the table that majority of management representatives from BHEL Shop Council (50.00 per cent) and TISCO JDC (60.64 per cent) stated that hierarchy in designation was taken as the criterion for the selection of members. But the workers; representatives from both the organizations stated that membership of elected union and discretion of the nominating authority were the bases of selection of members.

A majority of the management representatives of the middle and apex level from both the organizations stated that hierarchy in designation was the criterion followed for the nomination of members. Whereas the workers' representatives at the middle and the top levels stated that membership of the elected union is the criterion for the selection of members. A few members also stated that seniority in service and the ability to participate effectively ought to be the criteria in nominating members.

Table 3.2 : Criteria Followed for Nominating Members

(Members responses are indicated in percentage)

Criteria	BHEL						TISCO					
	Shop Council		*Joint Council*		*Joint Committee*		*Joint Departmental Council*		*Joint Works Council*		*Joint Consultative Council of Management*	
	M.R. N=24	W.R. N=24	M.R. N=4	W.R. N=4	M.R. N=2	W.R. N=2	M.R. N=94	W.R. N=94	M.R. N=2	W.R. N=2	M.R. N=2	W.R. N=2
Hierarchy in Designation	50.00	4.16	50.00	25.00	100.00	---	60.64	1.06	50.00	---	100.00	---
Seniority in Service	41.67	16.67	25.00	25.00	---	---	31.91	32.98	50.00	---	---	---
Member of elected union	---	50.00	---	50.00	---	100.00	---	31.92	---	100.00	---	100.00
Ability to participate effectively	---	12.50	---	---	---	---	4.26	---	---	---	---	---
Discretion of the nominating authority	8.33	16.67	25.00	---	---	---	3.19	34.04	---	---	---	---
Total	**100.00**	**100.00**	**100.00**	**100.00**	**100.00**	**100.00**	**100.00**	**100.00**	**100.00**	**100.00**	**100.00**	**100.00**

M.R. : Management Representatives; W.R. : Workers' Representatives **Source** : Data is collected through questionnaire.

A majority of the management representatives at all levels in both the organizations are of the opinion that hierarchy in designation is the criterion for nominating members. Whereas workers' representatives stated that seniority in service, membership of the elected union are the criteria for nominating members.

However, management representatives and employee representatives felt that the criteria followed at present are defective as they would not serve the purpose of participative management. Hence, they suggested a new criterion to be followed for nominating members based on purpose. Opinions of the members regarding the proposed criteria for nominating members are shown in Table 3.3. Some members expressed more than one opinion.

A majority of members from both the organizations at all levels stated that effectiveness in executing decisions should be the criterion for nominating members to the councils. Some members also expressed the view that efficiency in decision–making and experience as a members in various schemes should also be considered while nominating the management and worker representatives to the councils.

Thus, members suggested new bases for nomination like efficiency in decision–making and effectiveness in executing the decision, experience in various bodies etc., with a view to making participative management schemes effective.

But it is very difficult to follow these bases as there is no scale to measure efficiency in decision–making, effectiveness in executing decisions. Hence, it is suggested that bases like hierarchy in the designation may be followed as the criteria while giving some weightages to the efficiency in decision–making and execution.

c) Appointment of Chairman and Co–Chairman from among Worker and Management Representatives

It is observed from the above analysis that the Chairman is from among management representatives and the Co–Chairman from workers' representative in BHEL and the Chairmanship and Co–Chairmanship is by rotation from among management and worker representatives in TISCO. In view of the different practices in the two organizations and differences of preferences of representatives, the opinions of members regarding the holding the positions of Chairmanship and Co–Chairmanship are collected and presented in Table 3.4.

Table 3.3 : Desired Basis for Nomination—As Perceived by the Members

(Members responses are indicated in percentage)

Opinion	BHEL						TISCO					
	Shop Council		*Joint Council*		*Joint Committee*		*Joint Departmental Council*		*Joint Works Council*		*Joint Consultative Council of Management*	
	M.R. N=24	W.R. N=24	M.R. N=4	W.R. N=4	M.R. N=2	W.R. N=2	M.R. N=94	W.R. N=94	M.R. N=2	W.R. N=2	M.R. N=2	W.R. N=2
Efficiency in Decision-making	41.67	45.83	100.00	100.00	100.00	100.00	36.17	42.55	100.00	100.00	50.00	100.00
Experience as a member in various schemes	50.00	54.17	75.00	100.00	50.00	100.00	35.11	37.23	100.00	100.00	100.00	100.00
Effectiveness in executing decisions	62.50	75.00	100.00	50.00	100.00	100.00	63.83	69.15	50.00	100.00	50.00	50.00

M.R. : Management Representatives; W.R. : Workers' Representatives **Source** : Data is collected through questionnaire.

Note : Totals do not tally as each member expressed more than one opinion.

Table 3.4 : Preference of the Members Regarding Holding the Positions of Chairman and Vice–Chairman

(Members responses are indicated in percentage)

Preference	Chairman				Vice–Chairman			
	BHEL		*TISCO*		*BHEL*		*TISCO*	
	MR N=30	*WR* N=30	*MR* N=98	*WR* N=98	*MR* N=30	*WR* N=30	*MR* N=98	*WR* N=98
By Management representative	36.67	3.33	6.12	2.04	6.66	10.00	4.08	5.10
By workers representatives	10.00	30.00	4.08	6.12	36.67	16.67	10.20	4.08
By Rotation between the management and workers	53.33	66.67	89.90	91.84	56.67	73.33	85.72	90.82
Total	**100.00**	**100.00**	**100.00**	**100.00**	**100.00**	**100.00**	**100.00**	**100.00**

W.R. : Workers' Representative; M.R. : Management Representatives

Source : Information is collected through questionnaire.

It is observed from this table that a majority of the workers and management representatives at all levels in both the organizations stated that the positions of Chairman and Co–Chairman should be by rotation from among management and worker representatives every alternate years.

Hence, it is suggested that the management of BHEL should introduce the system of rotation and the management of TISCO can continue with the present system.

The tenure of office of the members is two years. Members who retire from the council are eligible for re-nomination. Any members nominated to fill a casual vacancy will hold office for the unexpired terms of his predecessor. The administrative body of the councils includes a secretary in addition to the Chairman and Co–Chairman. The secretary is elected by the Council. The secretary may or may not be a member of the Council, but should be an employee working in or attached to the department(s) covered by the Council. A non–member secretary will have no right to vote, but he can take part in the discussions of the Council[1].

The Councils have every right to co–opt, in a consultative capacity, persons employed in or attached to the department having special knowledge of any particular matter under discussion. For specific purposes, the Councils have a right to form sub–committees whose membership may extend beyond the membership of the Council.

Awareness and Interest of Participants

The success of workers' participation in management schemes depends largely upon the awareness of he members about the schemes as the awareness enhances the members' commitment to and involvement in the proceedings of the meetings. The other important factor influencing the success of the working is the interest of the members in the schemes which sustains the continuous and dedicated involvement of the members in the functioning of participative management schemes.

To make any scheme of participation successful, it is necessary that those who are involved in it should have a right idea about the concept of participative management and are aware of its functions and objectives. This enables the conduct of meetings systematically, raising relevant issues for discussion etc. It is also possible that a participant who himself is ill–informed, would not be able to communicate the objectives of the committees to his colleagues, and even if he ventures, he may do in a manner which leads to confusion. Since the participants in participative forums are the only link between the management and the labour.

The workers' genuine interest in any scheme of workers' participation in management is a must for its success and much emphasis has rightly been placed on it. Training the worker and developing in him an awareness of participative management are stressed to involve him in the process. But it is felt that not much has been achieved so far in this regard. As such the opinions of the members regarding the awareness of the concept of participative management were elicited and they are presented in Table 3.5.

The majority of the management representatives (37.50 per cent) from BHEL shop council perceived the concept as employee participa-

---

1. *Ibid.*

Table 3.5 : Perception of the Members about the Concept of Participative Management

(Members responses are indicated in percentage)

Members	BHEL						TISCO					
Perception about the concept of participative management	*Shop Council*		*Joint Council*		*Joint Committee*		*Joint Departmental Council*		*Joint Works Council*		*Joint Consultative Council of Management*	
	M.R. N=24	W.R. N=24	M.R. N=4	W.R. N=4	M.R. N=2	W.R. N=2	M.R. N=94	W.R. N=94	M.R. N=2	W.R. N=2	M.R. N=2	W.R. N=2
Informal Consultation	25.00	20.83	25.00	50.00	---	50.00	21.28	27.66	--	--	--	--
Formal Consultation	20.83	29.17	50.00	25.00	50.00	--	35.11	21.28	50.00	50.00	50.00	50.00
Information sharing	16.67	29.17	25.00	25.00	50.00	50.00	20.21	25.53	50.00	50.00	50.00	50.00
Employee Participation in Decision-making at Board Level	37.50	20.83	--	--	--	--	23.40	25.53	--	--	--	--
Total	**100.00**	**100.00**	**100.00**	**100.00**	**100.00**	**100.00**	**100.00**	**100.00**	**100.00**	**100.00**	**100.00**	**100.00**

M.R. : Management Representatives; W.R. : Workers' Representatives **Source** : Data is collected through questionnaire.

tion in decision–making at board level, whereas slightly less than one–third of the workers' representatives (29.17 per cent) from BHEL perceived the scheme as a formal consultation and information –sharing. But in TISCO more than one–third of the management representatives (35.11 per cent) perceived the concept as formal consultation. The scheme of participative management is an informal consultation as perceived by nearly one–fourth of the workers' representatives of TISCO's JDC.

At the middle level, the participative management is perceived by half of the management representatives from BHEL as a formal consultation. Contrary to this, the same number of workers' representatives from BHEL perceived the scheme an informal consultation. A unique opinion is observed from both the categories of representatives of TISCO as they perceived the scheme as formal consultation of information sharing.

At the apex level, the members from both the organizations perceived the scheme as a formal consultation and information–sharing.

It is also observed from the table that at the grass–root level, the members perceived the scheme as participation of employees in decision–making and formal consultation and informal consultation, whereas at middle level, the members perceived the scheme as formal consultation and information sharing. At the top level also, same opinion is observed among the members.

Thus, the majority of the members from both the organizations perceived the scheme as a device of formal consultation between the management and employees. However, it is viewed that some members do not have a clear conceptual idea. Hence, it is suggested that the management should educate the representatives about the concepts of participative management.

The members of the participative management should also known the objectives and functions of the participative management forums in addition to have an idea about the concept of participative management. The opinions of the members about their awareness regarding the functions and objectives are collected and presented in Table 3.6. It is observed from this table that majority of the management representatives (79.17 per cent) from BHEL's shop councils expressed the opinion that they are aware of the existence of participative management schemes after joining in the organization. Whereas nearly four–fifth of the workers' representatives (83.33 per cent) from BHEL stated that they are

Table 3.6 : Awareness of Respondents about the Functions and Objectives of Participative Management Forums

(Members responses are indicated in percentage)

Criteria	BHEL						TISCO					
	Shop Council		*Joint Council*		*Joint Committee*		*Joint Depart-mental Council*		*Joint Works Council*		*Joint Consul-tative Council of Management*	
	M.R. N=24	W.R. N=24	M.R. N=4	W.R. N=4	M.R. N=2	W.R. N=2	M.R. N=94	W.R. N=94	M.R. N=2	W.R. N=2	M.R. N=2	W.R. N=2
Aware before joining the organisation	4.17	--	50.00	--	100.00	--	30.85	21.28	100.00	50.00	100.00	50.00
Aware after the organization	79.17	16.67	50.00	100.00	--	100.00	64.90	53.19	--	50.00	--	50.00
Aware after becoming members in the committees	16.66	83.33	--	--	--	--	4.25	25.53	--	--	--	--
Total	**100.00**	**100.00**	**100.00**	**100.00**	**100.00**	**100.00**	**100.00**	**100.00**	**100.00**	**100.00**	**100.00**	**100.00**

M.R. : Management Representatives; W.R. : Workers' Representatives **Source** : Data is collected through questionnaire.

aware of the schemes only after becoming the members of the council. But nearly two–thirds of the management representatives (64.90 per cent) and a little over fifty per cent of the workers' representatives from TISCO shop council stated that they are aware of the schemes after joining the organization. A few members from both the organizations also expressed that they were aware of the scheme even before joining the organization.

The members are aware of the schemes after joining the organization as opined by fifty per cent of the management representatives and cent per cent worker representatives from BHEL joint council, whereas, cent per cent of the management representatives and fifty per cent of the workers' representatives from the JWC of TISCO expressed the opinion that they were aware of the schemes even before joining in the organization.

At the top level, almost all the management representatives from both the organizations stated that they were aware of the schemes even before joining the organization, whereas the workers' representatives to the tune of cent per cent from BHEL and fifty per cent from TISCO expressed that they become aware of the scheme only after joining the organization.

Inter–Council analysis shows that at all the levels almost all the categories of members have come to know of the schemes only after joining the organization.

It is also observed from the table that some members from TISCO were aware of the scheme before joining the organization whereas majority of the members from both the organizations are aware of the schemes only after joining the organization.

It is observed from the table 3.6 that majority of the members from both the organizations have had knowledge of participative management only after joining the organization. However, it is suggested that the management has to conduct awareness programmes for all the members about the scheme in order to make all the members and non–members know about different aspects of participative programme.

Members' awareness about the participative management can also be assessed based on the members' opinion regarding the need for participative management. The need for participative management can be attributed to several reasons. Members are asked to explain the need for participative management.

Table 3.7 shows members' opinion on the need for participative management. Majority of the management (66.67 per cent) and workers representatives (75.00 per cent) from BHEL shop council expressed that to encourage the upward communication, there is need for participative management. But majority of the management representatives (91.49 per cent) from TISCO's JDC expressed the opinion that the participative management is needed for effective implementation of decisions. Contrary to this, nearly four–fifths of the workers representatives (81.91 per cent) stated that to encourage the upward communication workers' participation in management is needed. The other reasons expressed by the members for the need for participative management are to contain resistance to change, to facilitate acceptable solution, to improve the quality of managerial decisions, to motivate the workers by instilling a sense of belonging and to promote leadership qualities among workers.

Cent per cent of management and workers' representatives at the middle level from both the organizations expressed the need for the scheme so as to encourage upward communication for effective implementation of decisions. Almost all the members have expressed the same reasons for the need for the participative management as expressed by the grass–root level members.

At the top level also, similar opinion is expressed by the members of both the organizations.

Council–wise analysis shows that the members of the lower levels perceived the need for participative management as a method to encourage the upward communication, whereas at the middle and apex levels the members perceived it as a tool to motivate the employees, for effective implementation of decisions etc.

But in both the organizations the majority of the members stated that participative management is essential to encourage upward communication.

Thus, the majority of the members are of the opinion that participative management is necessary to encourage the upward communication, to motivate the employees, and for effective implementation of decisions.

Workers' participation in management has been initiated by the Government through works committees. But the management alongwith the unions have started the workers' participation in management in some organizations. TISCO is the best example for such type of organization.

Table 3.7 : Need for Participative Management—As Viewed by the Members

(Members responses are indicated in percentage)

Opinion	BHEL						TISCO					
	Shop Council		*Joint Council*		*Joint Committee*		*Joint Departmental Council*		*Joint Works Council*		*Joint Consultative Council of Management*	
	M.R. N=24	W.R. N=24	M.R. N=4	W.R. N=4	M.R. N=2	W.R. N=2	M.R. N=94	W.R. N=94	M.R. N=2	W.R. N=2	M.R. N=2	W.R. N=2
To contain resistance to change	20.83	16.67	75.00	50.00	50.00	50.00	45.74	67.02	100.00	100.00	50.00	50.00
To facilitate acceptable solution	12.50	20.83	50.00	75.00	100.00	100.00	36.17	80.85	50.00	100.00	100.00	100.00
To satisfy employee ego	58.33	12.50	75.00	50.00	50.00	100.00	29.79	40.43	100.00	50.00	100.00	50.00
To encourage upward communication.	66.67	75.00	100.00	50.00	100.00	50.00	68.08	81.91	100.00	100.00	50.00	100.00
For effective implementation of the decision	37.50	70.83	100.00	100.00	50.00	50.00	91.49	41.49	100.00	100.00	50.00	50.00
To improve the quality of managerial decision	45.83	50.00	50.00	50.00	50.00	50.00	24.47	45.87	100.00	100.00	100.00	100.00
To motivate workers by insisting a sense of belonging	62.50	33.33	75.00	100.00	100.00	100.00	82.98	28.72	50.00	100.00	50.00	50.00
To promote leadership qualities among workers	25.00	29.17	25.00	50.00	50.00	50.00	20.21	32.98	50.00	50.00	50.00	100.00

M.R. : Management Representatives; W.R. : Workers' Representatives **Source** : Data is collected through questionnaire.

Totals do not tally as each member expressed more than one opinion.

Members awareness about the participative management also depends on their awareness about the initiated of the participative management schemes. Hence, an attempt has been made to enquire into the members perception about the parties promoted the participative management scheme in the organization. Table 3.8 shows the members' perception of the parties who are responsible for the promotion of the scheme in the respective organizations.

The majority of the management representatives (54.17 per cent) from the BHEL shop council expressed that the management of the organization initiated the schemes. Contrary to this, the workers' representatives (41.67 per cent each) opined that both the Government and Trade Unions took initiative in setting up the scheme, while nearly four–fifths of management representatives (82.98 per cent) and two–thirds of the workers' representatives (65.96 per cent) from TISCO's JDC stated that the management took the initiative in setting up the scheme.

At the middle level, the management representatives of BHEL opined that both the management and Government took initiative in the scheme, whereas the workers' representatives stated that both the Government and unions are the initiators of the scheme. Contrary to this, both the management and workers' representatives from TISCO's JWC stated that the management took the initiative in the scheme.

At the apex level the same kind of opinions were expressed in respect of both the organizations.

Organization–wise analysis shows that members in BHEL opined that management, Unions and Government have initiated the schemes, whereas in TISCO members viewed that the management took the initiative in the scheme.

Thus, it is observed that trade unions along with management took initiative in starting the participative scheme. In addition to the idea about the initiator, members should also know the degree of utility of the participative management forums. An attempt was made to find out the perceptions of the members of the degree of utility of the meetings. The members' perception of the level of utility of workers' participation in management is presented in Table 3.9.

Three–fourths of the management members (75.00 per cent) and just over half of the workers' representative (54.17 per cent) from BHEL shop council opined that the scheme of participative management is highly useful. And nearly four–fifths of the management representatives

Table 3.8 : Initiator of the Participative Management Schemes as Perceived by the Members

(Members responses are indicated in percentage)

Initiator	BHEL						TISCO					
	Shop Council		*Joint Council*		*Joint Committee*		*Joint Departmental Council*		*Joint Works Council*		*Joint Consultative Council of Management*	
	M.R. N=24	W.R. N=24	M.R. N=4	W.R. N=4	M.R. N=2	W.R. N=2	M.R. N=94	W.R. N=94	M.R. N=2	W.R. N=2	M.R. N=2	W.R. N=2
Government	33.33	41.67	50.00	50.00	50.00	50.00	--	--	--	--	--	--
Management	54.17	8.33	50.00	--	50.00	--	82.98	65.96	100.00	100.00	100.00	100.00
Trade Unions	--	41.67	--	50.00	--	50.00	5.32	23.40	--	--	--	--
All the parties	12.50	8.33	--	--	--	--	11.70	10.64	--	--	--	--
Total	**100.00**	**100.00**	**100.00**	**100.00**	**100.00**	**100.00**	**100.00**	**100.00**	**100.00**	**100.00**	**100.00**	**100.00**

M.R. : Management Representatives; W.R. : Workers' Representatives **Source** : Data is collected through questionnaire.

Table 3.9 : Utility of Participative Management as Perceived by Members

(Members responses are indicated in percentage)

Utility	BHEL						TISCO					
	Shop Council		*Joint Council*		*Joint Committee*		*Joint Departmental Council*		*Joint Works Council*		*Joint Consultative Council of Management*	
	M.R. N=24	W.R. N=24	M.R. N=4	W.R. N=4	M.R. N=2	W.R. N=2	M.R. N=94	W.R. N=94	M.R. N=2	W.R. N=2	M.R. N=2	W.R. N=2
Highly useful	75.00	54.17	75.00	50.00	100.00	100.00	84.04	68.08	100.00	100.00	100.00	100.00
Moderately useful	25.00	16.67	25.00	25.00	--	--	15.96	19.15	--	--	--	--
Not at all useful	--	29.16	--	25.00	--	--	--	12.77	--	--	--	--
Total	**100.00**	**100.00**	**100.00**	**100.00**	**100.00**	**100.00**	**100.00**	**100.00**	**100.00**	**100.00**	**100.00**	**100.00**

M.R. : Management Representatives; W.R. : Workers' Representatives **Source** : Data is collected through questionnaire.

(84.04 per cent) and 68.08 per cent of workers' representatives from TISCO also perceived that the scheme is highly useful. A few workers' representatives from both the organizations stated that the participative scheme are either moderately useful or not at all useful.

At the middle level also, the majority of the members from both the categories belonging the BHEL expressed that the schemes are highly useful. Cent per cent of the worker and management representatives from TISCO also opined the same.

Cent per cent of the members from both the organizations' apex level perceived that the schemes are highly useful.

Organization–wise analysis shows that more members from TISCO have perceived that the scheme is highly useful than those from BHEL.

The members who described the utility of the participative management as high and moderate were asked about the beneficiaries of the scheme. The opinions of the members are presented in the Table 3.10.

The majority of the management representatives (58.33 per cent) from BHEL shop council perceived that both the management and employees are the beneficiaries of the scheme. Similarly, slightly more than two–thirds of the workers' representatives (70.59 per cent) from BHEL were of the same opinion. Contrary to this, 39.36 per cent of the management representatives and half of the workers' representatives from TISCO's JDC perceived that both the parties are beneficiaries of the scheme. Some members from both the organizations also expressed that all the parties are beneficiaries of the scheme.

As far as the middle level is concerned both the management representatives and workers' representatives from both the organizations felt that all the parties, i.e., employees, management and society are the beneficiaries of the scheme. Similar opinion is expressed by the members of the apex council from both the organizations.

To sum up, the majority of the members from shop council expressed that both the management and employees are beneficiaries and members from middle and apex council expressed that all the parties including the society are beneficiaries of the scheme.

The above analysis indicates that most of the members have awareness about the concept, objectives, functions, need, and utility of the participative management schemes. However, it is suggested that the management should educate the other members through training programmes and supply of literature on participative management forums.

Table 3.10 : Beneficiaries of Participative Management as Perceived by the Members

(Members responses are indicated in percentage)

Beneficiaries	BHEL						TISCO					
	Shop Council		*Joint Council*		*Joint Committee*		*Joint Departmental Council*		*Joint Works Council*		*Joint Consultative Council of Management*	
	M.R. N=24	W.R. N=24	M.R. N=4	W.R. N=4	M.R. N=2	W.R. N=2	M.R. N=94	W.R. N=94	M.R. N=2	W.R. N=2	M.R. N=2	W.R. N=2
Employees	12.50	5.88	--	--	--	--	17.02	8.54	--	--	--	--
Management	12.50	--	--	--	--	--	13.83	23.17	--	--	--	--
Both Management and Employees	58.34	70.59	25.00	33.33	--	--	39.36	50.00	--	--	--	--
Society	8.33	--	--	--	--	--	7.45	1.22	--	--	--	--
All the above	8.33	23.53	75.00	66.67	100.00	100.00	22.34	17.07	100.00	100.00	100.00	100.00
Total	**100.00**	**100.00**	**100.00**	**100.00**	**100.00**	**100.00**	**100.00**	**100.00**	**100.00**	**100.00**	**100.00**	**100.00**

M.R. : Management Representatives; W.R. : Workers' Representatives **Source** : Data is collected through questionnaire.

The members should also be interested in the participative management forums in addition to having awareness in order to participate in the forums effectively. The opinions of the members about their interest in the scheme were collected and are presented in table 3.11. It is observed from the table that the majority of the members i.e., 70.83 per cent management and 87.50 per cent workers' representatives from BHEL shop council expressed schemes. As far as the responses from TISCO's JDC is concerned, more than four–fifths of the management (87.23 per cent) and workers' (89.36 per cent) representatives stated that they are very much interested in the schemes of participative management. An insignificant number of employees from both the organizations stated that they are moderately/not at all interested in the scheme.

At the middle and apex levels also cent per cent of the members of both the categories from both the organizations viewed that they are highly interested in the scheme.

It is also observed from the Table 3.11 that among the representatives who evince interest in the scheme, worker representatives out number the management representatives in both the organizations.

To sum up, the majority of the employees from both the organizations expressed that they are highly interested in the scheme. The management of both the organizations should provide necessary training to create interest among the members as there are some members who have no interest.

Working of the Scheme

Effective functioning of the scheme of workers' participation in management is most essential as huge financial and human resources are involved in the process of functioning of the schemes and as it contributes to the successful attainment of organizational goals.

The working of participative management can be assessed on the basis of the effectiveness in preparation of agenda, conduct of meeting regularly, encouraging all the members to attend the meetings, conducting the proceedings of the meetings seriously and sincerely, following participative approach in discussion of various issues, making decisions through consensus approach and implementing all the agreed decisions without serious time lapse.

1. Preparation of Agenda

Preparation of agenda plays a vital role in participative manage-

Table 3.11 : Interest of the Parties in the Participative Management Schemes

(Members responses are indicated in percentage)

Interest	BHEL						TISCO					
	Shop Council		*Joint Council*		*Joint Committee*		*Joint Departmental Council*		*Joint Works Council*		*Joint Consultative Council of Management*	
	M.R. N=24	W.R. N=24	M.R. N=4	W.R. N=4	M.R. N=2	W.R. N=2	M.R. N=94	W.R. N=94	M.R. N=2	W.R. N=2	M.R. N=2	W.R. N=2
Highly Interested	70.83	87.50	100.00	100.00	100.00	100.00	87.23	89.36	100.00	100.00	100.00	100.00
Moderately Interested	25.00	8.33	--	--	--	--	9.58	6.38	--	--	--	--
Not at all interested	4.17	4.17	--	--	--	--	3.19	4.26	--	--	--	--
Total	**100.00**	**100.00**	**100.00**	**100.00**	**100.00**	**100.00**	**100.00**	**100.00**	**100.00**	**100.00**	**100.00**	**100.00**

M.R. : Management Representatives; W.R. : Workers' Representatives **Source** : Data is collected through questionnaire.

ment. Agenda–preparation, to be effective, should be based on the issues proposed by the members and non–members, finalization of issues by mutual consultation between the members. Once the agenda is finalized, it should be communicated to all the members without fail. It is needless to say that the notice of the meetings should be sent to all the members in time.

Normally members, based on their experiences and practical knowledge of affairs, identify the weak points in the production, organization etc., and proposed such issues for inclusion in the agenda in order to exchange their experience with other members in the forum. Table 3.12 depicts the total number of items proposed by the members at each level of the participative management in BHEL and TISCO. It is observed from this table that 186 members of shop councils in BHEL proposed 1,939 issues (10.42 issues per member). Whereas 694 members proposed 6.846 issues (9.86 issues per member) in TISCO's JDC.

At the middle level, 281 issues were proposed by 14 members (6.39 issues per member) in BHEL and 380 issues were proposed by 26 members in TISCO. As far as the apex level is concerned, in BHEL, 18 members proposed 170 issues (9.44 issues per member), whereas in TISCO 22 members proposed 450 issues (20.45 issues per member).

Thus it is clear from the table 3.12 that the members of BHEL at shop council are active compared to those of TISCO in proposing number of items. On the other hand, the members of TISCO at middle and apex levels are active compared to those of BHEL. Hence, it is suggested that the members should also be contacted and encouraged to propose all their issues without any shyness or hesitation.

Frequency of Proposal of Issues

The opinions of members regarding the frequency of proposing issues can help us in deciding the extent of interest of members in making use of this machinery. Frequency of proposal of issues by the members is presented in Table 3.13. It is observed from this table that more than 60.00 per cent of the management representatives and two–thirds of the workers' representatives from BHEL shop council and more than 70 per cent of the management representatives and 69.15 per cent workers' representatives from TISCO's JDC expressed the opinion that they frequently propose issues.

It is also observed from the table 3.13 fifty per cent of the management representatives from the joint council of BHEL opined that

Table 3.12 : Issues Proposed and Included in the Agenda during 1987–88

Level of Council	BHEL			TISCO		
	Number of Issues proposed	*Issues included in Agenda*	*Percentage proposed*	*Number of Issues proposed*	*Issues included in Agenda*	*Percentage proposed*
Gross–root level	1,939	1,105	56.99	6,846	4,213	61.54
Middle Level	281	180	64.06	380	256	67.37
Apex Level	170	120	70.58	450	346	76.89
Total	**2,390**	**1,405**		**7,676**	**4,815**	

Source: Compiled from the Minutes of Participative councils of BHEL & TISCO

they frequently present issues at meetings. Contrary to this, same percentage (50) of the workers' representatives from BHEL stated that they now and then propose issues to the agenda committee. As far as the TISCO's JWC is concerned, cent per cent of the management representatives and fifty per cent of the workers' representatives stated that they frequently represent issues to the meetings.

At the apex level, same opinion was expressed by all the members in both the organizations regarding proposal of the issue at meetings. They stated that they are frequently proposing issues.

Council–wise analysis shows that lower level and apex level council members frequently represent issues at the meetings in BHEL, but all the council members contribute significantly in TISCO.

Organization–wise analysis shows that less than two–thirds of the members from BHEL stated that they propose issues frequently, whereas more than two–thirds of the members from TISCO observed that they frequently propose issues. It is clear that more than one–third of the members do not propose issues frequently.

It is, therefore, suggested that the management of BHEL, and more so TISCO, should encourage the members at the middle level to propose issues frequently.

The management should know the reasons for lethargy on the part of the members in proposing the issues before taking steps to correct the situation. An attempt was made to ascertain the reasons for not proposing

Table 3.13 : Frequency of Proposal of Issues by the Members

(Members responses are indicated in percentage)

Frequency	BHEL						TISCO					
	Shop Council		*Joint Council*		*Joint Committee*		*Joint Depart-mental Council*		*Joint Works Council*		*Joint Consul-tative Council of Management*	
	M.R. N=24	W.R. N=24	M.R. N=4	W.R. N=4	M.R. N=2	W.R. N=2	M.R. N=94	W.R. N=94	M.R. N=2	W.R. N=2	M.R. N=2	W.R. N=2
Frequently	62.50	66.67	50.00	25.00	100.00	100.00	73.40	69.15	100.00	50.00	100.00	50.00
Now and then	20.83	8.33	25.00	50.00	--	--	17.02	11.70	--	50.00	--	50.00
Never	16.67	25.00	25.00	25.00	--	--	9.58	19.15	--	--	--	--
Total	**100.00**	**100.00**	**100.00**	**100.00**	**100.00**	**100.00**	**100.00**	**100.00**	**100.00**	**100.00**	**100.00**	**100.00**

M.R. : Management Representatives; W.R. : Workers' Representatives **Source** : Data is collected through questionnaire.

any issue from those who did not do so. Table 3.14 shows the reasons, therefore. It is observed from the table that at the lower level, three–fourths of the management representatives from BHEL and around two–thirds of management representatives from TISCO do not have any issues of management representatives from TISCO do not have any issues to propose in the meetings. Contrary to this, two–thirds of the worker members expressed that they propose the issues to the suggestions scheme and as such they do not propose issues to the council[1]. One third of the management representatives of TISCO stated that they lack the opportunity to initiate the issues in the meetings. Lack of opportunity to initiate (one–third) and proposing the issues to the suggestion scheme (one–third) are the reasons expressed by the workers' representatives for not proposing issues to the council. A few workers' representatives pointed out that the negative attitude of the management is the reason for not proposing the issues. Only one management representative from BHEL joint council observed that there was no issue to propose at the meetings.

It is clear from the table that the reasons for members not being active in this case are existence of suggestion schemes and the negative attitude of the management. Hence, it is suggested that the management should offer an in–built incentives in the participative scheme in addition to creating a positive environment and a opportunity to enable the members to propose the issues.

Nature of Issues

Proposing too many issues frequently may not contribute to the success of the participative management scheme as some of the issues proposed by the members may not be worth of discussion. Hence, an attempt was made to find out the nature of the issues proposed by the members. Table 3.15 shows nature of issues proposed by the members.

It is observed from the table 3.15 that the majority of the management representatives (60.00 per cent) and half of the workers' representatives from BHEL's shop council expressed that they proposed issues relating to production. Besides production, the members (both) proposed issues concerning welfare, safety and personnel. Contrary to this, a little over one–third of the management representatives from TISCO JDC

1. Suggestions Schemes is in existence in both the organizations. The workers will be paid reward and a merit certificate when they suggest any item for the growth of the organization.

Table 3.14 : Reasons for not Proposing any Issue

(Members responses are indicated in percentage)

Reasons	BHEL						TISCO					
	Shop Council		*Joint Council*		*Joint Committee*		*Joint Departmental Council*		*Joint Works Council*		*Joint Consultative Council of Management*	
	M.R. N=24	W.R. N=24	M.R. N=4	W.R. N=4	M.R. N=2	W.R. N=2	M.R. N=94	W.R. N=94	M.R. N=2	W.R. N=2	M.R. N=2	W.R. N=2
Lack of opportunity to initiate	25.00	33.33	--	--	--	--	44.44	33.33	--	--	--	--
Negative attitude of Management	--	16.67	--	--	--	--	--	22.22	--	--	--	--
No issues to propose	75.00	16.67	100.00	--	--	--	55.56	11.11	--	--	--	--
Existence of suggestion schemes	--	33.33	--	--	--	--	--	33.33	--	--	--	--
Total	**100.00**	**100.00**	**100.00**				**100.00**	**100.00**				

M.R. : Management Representatives; W.R. : Workers' Representatives **Source** : Data is collected through questionnaire.

Table 3.15 : Nature of Issues Proposed by the Members

(*Members responses are indicated in percentage*)

Nature	BHEL						TISCO					
	Shop Council		*Joint Council*		*Joint Committee*		*Joint Depart-mental Council*		*Joint Works Council*		*Joint Consul-tative Council of Management*	
	M.R. N=24	W.R. N=24	M.R. N=4	W.R. N=4	M.R. N=2	W.R. N=2	M.R. N=94	W.R. N=94	M.R. N=2	W.R. N=2	M.R. N=2	W.R. N=2
Production and Productivity	60.00	50.00	100.00	33.33	50.00	--	29.41	19.74	100.00	--	50.00	50.00
Welfare	30.00	22.22	--	66.67	--	100.00	37.65	17.11	--	100.00	50.00	50.00
Safety	--	16.67	--	--	--	--	21.18	48.68	--	--	--	--
Finance	--	--	--	--	50.00	--	--	--	--	--	--	--
Personnel	10.00	11.11	--	--	--	--	11.76	14.47	--	--	--	--
Total	**100.00**	**100.00**	**100.00**	**100.00**	**100.00**	**100.0**	**100.00**	**100.00**	**100.00**	**100.00**	**100.00**	**100.00**

M.R. : Management Representatives; W.R. : Workers' Representatives **Source** : Data is collected through questionnaire.

expressed that most of the issues proposed by them concerned welfare. But the majority of the workers representatives (48.68 per cent) from TISCO expressed that safety issues take the lion's share in the total issues proposed by them. Other members also expressed that they proposed items relating to production, personnel etc.

As far as the middle level councils are concerned, issues relating to production and welfare in both the organizations were referred frequently. At the apex level also all the members from both the organizations expressed that the nature of issues they proposed was related to production and welfare.

It is further observed from the table that at the lower level, the majority of the members proposed the issues relating to production, while production and welfare issues were referred to at the middle level, and the issues related to production, welfare, finance were proposed at top level.

It is thus found that most of the issues referred to are related to important items like production and welfare. However certain issues which are not covered by the participative management scheme like personnel are also proposed in the meetings. It is, therefore suggested that the management should educate the members regarding the issues to be proposed.

Representations from Non–Members

The majority of the employees in the organization are not members of the participative forums. Though the non–members are not directly involved in the forums, their suggestions are very valuable to the members of the forums. The activity of the non–members in representing the issues also improves the activity of the members. Non–members send the issues to the members of the forum concerned for consideration and inclusion in the agenda. Hence, members were asked about the frequency of representations from non–members. Table 3.16 shows the frequency of representations from non–members.

It is observed from this table that 68.37 per cent of the members from TISCO and 61.67 per cent of the members from BHEL stated that they receive frequent representations from the non–members. A few members expressed that they did not receive any representations from the non–members.

As far as the shop council of BHEL is concerned 70.83 per cent of the management representatives and 58.33 per cent of the workers

Table 3.16 : Frequency of Representations from Non–members

(Members responses are indicated in percentage)

Frequency	BHEL						TISCO					
	Shop Council		*Joint Council*		*Joint Committee*		*Joint Depart-mental Council*		*Joint Works Council*		*Joint Consul-tative Council of Management*	
	M.R. N=24	W.R. N=24	M.R. N=4	W.R. N=4	M.R. N=2	W.R. N=2	M.R. N=94	W.R. N=94	M.R. N=2	W.R. N=2	M.R. N=2	W.R. N=2
Frequent representations	70.83	58.34	25.00	50.00	50.00	100.00	68.08	67.02	100.00	50.00	100.00	100.00
Representing now and then	20.84	20.83	50.00	50.00	50.00	--	23.40	22.34	--	--	--	--
No represen-tation	8.33	20.83	25.00	--	--	--	8.52	10.64	--	50.00	--	--
Total	**100.00**	**100.00**	**100.00**	**100.00**	**100.00**	**100.00**	**100.00**	**100.00**	**100.00**	**100.00**	**100.00**	**100.00**

M.R. : Management Representatives; W.R. : Workers' Representatives. **Source** : Data is collected through questionnaire.

representatives observed that the non–members in their organization frequently represent to the councils. Similar opinion were expressed by majority of the representatives of TISCO (68.08 per cent management and 67.02 per cent worker). Some members from both the organizations opined that the non–members represent to the councils now and then. Ten per cent of the members from the two organizations expressed that they never received any representation from the non–members.

The non–members proposes the issues now and then, as expressed by most of the management and workers' representatives (50.00 per cent) from BHEL joint council. Contrary to this almost all the members from TISCO's JWC stated that the non–members are frequently representing to the councils. At the apex level the majority of the members (75.00 per cent) from BHEL and all the members from TISCO observed that there is frequent representations from the non–members.

Inter–council analysis shows that the lower level members from BHEL receive frequent representations from non–members, whereas in TISCO the non–members at all levels represent to the members frequently. Hence, it is suggested that the management of BHEL should educate and create awareness among all employees about the importance and utility of representing the issues to the members of participative management.

The importance of the suggestions from the non–members depends on the nature of issues they present to the councils. The nature of issues represented to members by non–members was collected from members and is presented in the Table 3.17. It is observed from the table that majority of the management and workers' representatives from the shop council of BHEL and JDC of TISCO opined that they received representations from non–members on all the issues viz., production, safety, welfare and personnel.

As far as middle level councils are concerned, more than 65.00 per cent of the management representatives and 75.00 per cent workers' representatives from BHEL stated that the nature of representations from the non–members related to production and all the issues (viz., production, safety, finance, personnel etc.) respectively. At the apex level also the members opined that they received representations from non–members on various significant items.

It is clear from this table that almost all the non–members presented important issues which come under the scope of participative management. The management should keep up the same tempo in this regard.

Table 3.17 : Nature of Issues Received from Non-members

(Members responses are indicated in percentage)

Issues	BHEL						TISCO					
	Shop Council		*Joint Council*		*Joint Committee*		*Joint Departmental Council*		*Joint Works Council*		*Joint Consultative Council of Management*	
	M.R. N=24	W.R. N=24	M.R. N=4	W.R. N=4	M.R. N=2	W.R. N=2	M.R. N=94	W.R. N=94	M.R. N=2	W.R. N=2	M.R. N=2	W.R. N=2
Production	9.09	15.79	66.67	--	50.00	--	8.14	9.52	--	--	--	--
Safety	9.09	10.53	--	25.00	--	--	12.79	9.52	--	--	--	--
Welfare	13.64	10.53	33.33	--	--	--	9.30	8.33	50.00	--	50.00	--
Individual/ Personal Problems	--	5.26	--	--	--	--	8.14	4.76	--	--	--	--
All the above	68.18	57.89	--	75.00	50.00	100.00	66.63	67.86	50.00	100.00	50.00	100.00
Total	**100.00**	**100.00**	**100.00**	**100.00**	**100.00**	**100.00**	**100.00**	**100.00**	**100.00**	**100.00**	**100.00**	**100.00**

M.R. : Management Representatives; W.R. : Workers' Representatives **Source** : Data is collected through questionnaire.

Table 3.18 presents the reasons for non–inclusion of all the proposed issues in the agenda. It is observed from this table that majority of the management representatives (50.00 per cent) from BHEL shop council perceived that the insignificant nature of he issues was the reason for the non–inclusion of all the issues was the reason for the non–inclusion of all the issues on the agenda. The majority of the worker representatives (54.17 per cent) stated that the issues proposed were beyond the scope of the participative councils. The other reason for non–inclusion of the proposed issues, as per the members of BHEL shop council was the coverage of the issues already on the agenda. Most of the members from both the categories in (53.19 per cent of management and 40.42 per cent of workers' representatives in TISCO) expressed that proposal of too many issues was the reason for non–inclusion of all the issues on the agenda.

At the middle and top levels almost all the categories of members from both the organizations expressed the proposal of issues beyond the scope of the council was the reason.

This table also reveals that the important reasons for non–inclusion are partly due to offering of issues, which are beyond the scope of participative management and partly due to their insignificance. Hence, it is suggested that the management should educate the members to offer significant issues and those which are within the scope of participative management. It is further suggested that the advisory committee should take all precautions in eliminating issues as it discourages the members from proposing issues.

The appropriate body, after receiving the proposals prepares the agenda, mostly by mutual consultations. Mutual consultations not only help the members to include worthy issues but also minimize the discouragement on the part of those members whose issues are not recorded. But some times, the agenda is prepared by the chairman or the deputy chairman without mutual consultations. This type of practice demotivates the members.

The Secretary/Chairman of the councils in BHEL draws up the agenda for the meeting and issues the same to the members one week in advance. Any suggestions or comments on the agenda items are taken up during the deliberations of the council.

There is a separate sub–committee for the preparation of the agenda in TISCO. The agenda sub–committee is constituted by the JDC's with

Table 3.18 : Reasons for Non-inclusion of all the Proposed Issues on the Agenda

(Members responses are indicated in percentage)

Reason	BHEL						TISCO					
	Shop Council		*Joint Council*		*Joint Committee*		*Joint Departmental Council*		*Joint Works Council*		*Joint Consultative Council of Management*	
	M.R. N=24	W.R. N=24	M.R. N=4	W.R. N=4	M.R. N=2	W.R. N=2	M.R. N=94	W.R. N=94	M.R. N=2	W.R. N=2	M.R. N=2	W.R. N=2
Too many items	--	--	--	--	--	--	53.19	40.42	--	100.00	--	--
Beyond the scope	37.50	54.17	--	50.00	100.00	100.00	31.91	39.36	100.00	--	100.00	100.00
Already covered	12.50	8.33	100.00	--	--	--	3.19	2.13	--	--	--	--
Insignificant	50.00	37.50	--	50.00	--	--	11.71	18.09	--	--	--	--
Total	**100.00**	**100.00**	**100.00**	**100.00**	**100.00**	**100.00**	**100.00**	**100.00**	**100.00**	**100.00**	**100.00**	**100.00**

M.R. : Management Representatives; W.R. : Workers' Representatives **Source** : Data is collected through questionnaire.

an equal number of representatives from management and employees. These representatives are elected from among the members of the council itself and their term of office is one year. The secretary of the council serves as convener of the sub–committee[1]. If sufficient number of issues does not come up from the shop floor, members of the agenda sub–committee take the initiative in stimulating employees to offer suggestions. At the time of preparing the agenda, the sub–committee carefully scrutinizes and examines all the suggestions received, and if admissible, includes them for consideration at the next meeting or at a subsequent meeting. When it is decided not to include a particular suggestion the member of the agenda committee should explain to the worker the reason why his suggestion was not included so that he may feel that his suggestion received proper consideration and thus won't feel discouraged from making any suggestion in the future[2].

Against this background an attempt was made to enquire into the practice of finalizing the agenda. Table 3.19 shows the opinions of the members on the practice of preparation of agenda. It is observed from this table that half of the worker representatives of BHEL shop council expressed that the Chairman prepares the agenda for the meetings, while two–thirds of the management representatives belonging to BHEL shop councils stated that the agenda for the meeting is prepared by the members by mutual consultation. Contrary to this, both the categories of members (70.21 per cent of management and 42.55 per cent of workers' representatives) from TISCO's JDC expressed that agenda sub–committee, by mutual consultation, prepares the agenda for the meetings. Less than fifty per cent of the worker representatives from BHEL also stated that the members of the council by mutual consultation prepares the agenda for the meetings.

As far as the joint councils in BHEL are concerned, three–fourths of the management representatives stated that the agenda for the meetings is prepared by the members by mutual consultation. But, fifty per cent of the workers' representatives differed from the opinion of the management representatives by stating that the chairman of the council prepares the agenda for the meetings. But cent per cent of the members.

There is difference of opinion among the members of BHEL's apex level on the preparation of the agenda. All the management representatives stated that the agenda is finalized by consulting all the members,

1. Tata Steel, Constitution of Joint Committees of Joint Consultations, p. 17.
2. *Ibid.*

Table 3.19 : Reasons for Non-inclusion of all the Proposed Issues on the Agenda

(Members responses are indicated in percentage)

Person Preparing the Agenda	BHEL						TISCO					
	Shop Council		*Joint Council*		*Joint Committee*		*Joint Departmental Council*		*Joint Works Council*		*Joint Consultative Council of Management*	
	M.R. N=24	W.R. N=24	M.R. N=4	W.R. N=4	M.R. N=2	W.R. N=2	M.R. N=94	W.R. N=94	M.R. N=2	W.R. N=2	M.R. N=2	W.R. N=2
Chairman	29.17	50.00	25.00	50.00	--	100.00	27.66	40.42	--	--	--	--
Deputy Chairman	4.16	8.33	--	25.00	--	--	2.13	17.02	--	--	--	--
Members by actual consultation	66.67	41.67	75.00	25.00	100.00	--	70.21	42.56	100.00	100.00	100.00	100.00
Total	**100.00**	**100.00**	**100.00**	**100.00**	**100.00**	**100.00**	**100.00**	**100.00**	**100.00**	**100.00**	**100.00**	**100.00**

M.R. : Management Representatives; W.R. : Workers' Representatives. **Source** : Data is collected through questionnaire.

whereas the workers' representatives stated that the agenda is finalized by the Chairman himself. There is a common opinion among the members (both) in TISCO that the agenda is prepared by mutual consultations.

It may be viewed from this table that agenda is finalized mostly by mutual consultations. However, a significant number of members reported that the chairman or deputy chairman also prepared the agenda without consulting the members which is against the principles of participative management. Hence, it is suggested to both the organizations that the management should caution the Chairman or the Deputy Chairman of the schemes against such practices.

Circulation of Agenda

The Secretary concerned of the council should send the agenda, after its preparation, to all the members in time. But the practical difficulties hinder this practice some times which endangers the working of the scheme. Hence, the members were asked to explain the regularity in receiving the agenda in time.

Table 3.20 shows the opinions of the members about the regularity in receiving the agenda in time. It is observed from the table that more than two–thirds of the members from TISCO expressed that they received the agenda regularly in time. As far as BHEL is concerned, less than fifty per cent of the members opined the same.

The majority of the management representatives (54.17 per cent) from the shop council of BHEL expressed that the agenda is circulated among the members in time. Contrary to this, most of the workers representatives (50.00 per cent) stated that they received the agenda in time some times only. There is almost the same opinion among both the categories of members (76.60 per cent management and 69.15 per cent of worker) of JDC of TISCO. A few members from both the organizations expressed that they never received the agenda in time.

As far as the joint council in BHEL is concerned the agenda is circulated among the members in time, as expressed by three–fourths of the management representatives from BHEL. But fifty per cent of the workers' representatives differed from the management representatives' opinion by stating that only some times the agenda is circulated in time. All the management and workers' representatives from TISCO's JWC expressed that they received the agenda in time regularly.

At the apex level all the members from both the organizations opined that the agenda is being circulated regularly in time among members.

Table 3.20: Regularity in the Receipt of Agenda in Time

(Members responses are indicated in percentage)

Regularity	BHEL						TISCO					
	Shop Council		*Joint Council*		*Joint Committee*		*Joint Departmental Council*		*Joint Works Council*		*Joint Consultative Council of Management*	
	M.R. N=24	W.R. N=24	M.R. N=4	W.R. N=4	M.R. N=2	W.R. N=2	M.R. N=94	W.R. N=94	M.R. N=2	W.R. N=2	M.R. N=2	W.R. N=2
Always	54.17	41.67	75.00	25.00	100.00	100.00	76.60	69.15	100.00	100.00	100.00	100.00
Sometimes	37.50	50.00	25.00	50.00	--	--	19.15	23.40	--	--	--	--
Never	8.33	8.33	--	25.00	--	--	4.25	7.45	--	--	--	--
Total	**100.00**	**100.00**	**100.00**	**100.00**	**100.00**	**100.00**	**100.00**	**100.00**	**100.00**	**100.00**	**100.00**	**100.00**

M.R. : Management Representatives; W.R. : Workers' Representatives. **Source** : Data is collected through questionnaire.

It is further observed from the table that the agenda is being circulated to the members in time in TISCO rather than in BHEL, according to the opinion of the members.

If the agenda is not circulated in time, it will cause inconvenience and confusion to the members. Hence, the members who did not receive the agenda in time were enquired about the reasons for not receiving the agenda in time with a view to suggesting measures to circulate the agenda in time. Table 3.21 shows the reasons for the same.

It is observed from the table that an equal number of management and workers' representatives from BHEL shop council (50.00 per cent) stated that the reason for non–receipt of agenda was absence of sincerity of the secretarial staff of the Chairman. The members also stated that because of the negligent attitude of the management and non–availability of the member in the seat the agenda was not circulated in time. As far as TISCO is concerned the majority of the management representatives expressed that at the time of circulation of agenda, they may not have been available in their seat. But most of the workers' representatives opined that because of the indifferent attitude of the secretarial staff of the chairman, the agenda was not circulated in time.

Most of the members from BHEL (60.00 per cent) and TISCO (45.45 per cent) has stated the reason for non–receipt of the agenda in time is the indifferent attitude of the secretarial staff.

The reasons identified by the workers for non–receipt of the agenda are negative attitude of the management and the indifferent attitude of the secretarial staff. This type of practice should not be tolerated by the chairman of the council. The chairman should take steps to inculcate seriousness among the staff and circulate the agenda regularly in time.

2. Meetings Held : Notices of the Meetings

As per the norms of the Government, the notice of the meeting should reach the members seven days in advance of the meeting. The organizations have also framed rules and regulations accordingly. A notice of every meeting is sent to the members in BHEL one week in advance[1]. The dates of the meetings in TISCO are prefixed[2]. The secretary of the council also sends the notice of the meetings to the members. But it is not necessary in case of TISCO as the dates of meetings are prefixed and are intimated to the members. Table 3.22 shows the

1. BHEL., "Power to the people through participation", *op. cit*, p. 2.
2. Tata Steel, Constitution of the Joint Committees of Joint Consultation, p. 14.

Table 3.21 : Reasons for Non-receipt of Agenda in Time

(Members responses are indicated in percentage)

Reason	BHEL						TISCO					
	Shop Council		*Joint Council*		*Joint Committee*		*Joint Departmental Council*		*Joint Works Council*		*Joint Consultative Council of Management*	
	M.R. N=2	W.R. N=2	M.R.	W.R. N=1	M.R.	W.R.	M.R.	W.R. N=7	M.R.	W.R.	M.R.	W.R.
Negligent attitude of Management	--	50.00	--	--	--	--	--	28.57	--	--	--	--
Non-availability of the member	50.00	--	--	--	--	--	75.00	14.29	--	--	--	--
Indifferent attitude of the secretarial staff of the chairman	50.00	50.00	--	100.00	--	--	25.00	57.14	--	--	--	--
Total	**100.00**	**100.00**	**--**	**100.00**	**--**	**--**	**100.00**	**100.00**	**--**	**--**	**--**	**--**

M.R. : Management Representatives; W.R. : Workers' Representatives **Source** : Data is collected through questionnaire.

Table 3.22 : Regularity in Receipt of Notices of Meetings

(*Members responses are indicated in percentage*)

Regularity	BHEL						TISCO					
	Shop Council		*Joint Council*		*Joint Committee*		*Joint Departmental Council*		*Joint Works Council*		*Joint Consultative Council of Management*	
	M.R. N=24	W.R. N=24	M.R. N=4	W.R. N=4	M.R. N=2	W.R. N=2	M.R. N=94	W.R. N=94	M.R. N=2	W.R. N=2	M.R. N=2	W.R. N=2
Always	75.00	79.17	75.00	25.00	100.00	100.00	100.00	100.00	100.00	100.00	100.00	100.00
Sometimes	16.67	12.50	25.00	75.00	--	--	--	--	--	--	--	--
Never	8.33	8.33	--	--	--	--	--	--	--	--	--	--
Total	**100.00**	**100.00**	**100.00**	**100.00**	**100.00**	**100.00**	**100.00**	**100.00**	**100.00**	**100.00**	**100.00**	**100.00**

M.R. : Management Representatives; W.R. : Workers' Representatives. **Source** : Data is collected through questionnaire.

regularity in receiving the notices of the meetings by the members of the BHEL.

It is observed from the table 3.22 that more than three–fourths of the members from BHEL shop council opined that they received notices of the meetings regularly. A few members from BHEL's shop council also expressed that only some times they received the notices of the meetings.

The majority of the management representatives from BHEL joint council expressed that the notices of the meetings are received regularly. Contrary to this the notices of the meetings are received only some times, as stated by the workers' representatives.

As far as the apex councils are concerned, notices of the meetings are issued regularly, as opined by both the categories of members.

There is difference of opinion among the members of shop council and joint council of BHEL in respect of issuing notices of the meetings. There are cases of non–receipt of notices about the meetings in BHEL. The above analysis shows that some times certain members did not receive notices regularly. There are some instances of not receiving notices at all. The reasons identified by the members for this trend are the negative attitude of the chairman, the indifferent attitude of the secretarial staff, and communication barriers. It is, therefore, suggested that the secretary of the council should be utmost serious in sending notices of meetings to all the members in time. He should obtain feedback from the members regarding the receipt of the notices and the agenda.

3. Members' Attendance

Normally, the members, after receiving the agenda and the notice of the meeting, attend the meeting and discuss the issues. But some of the members some times may not attend the meetings owing to various reasons. The BHEL management has appealed to its members of the council that it is necessary that all members of the council attend all meetings without fail. Should they wish to abstain from any meeting, they shall obtain permission from the chairman of the council[1]. A similar appeal was also made to the members by the management of TISCO. The management of TISCO provides on–duty leave for attending the meetings of the council[2]. The high rate of incidence of absenteeism in the meetings reduces the interest of the chairman and other members. Percentage of attendance of the members at the meetings (Table 3.23)

1. BHEL, Personnel Manual, p. 6.6.9.
2. Tata Steel, Constitutions of Joint Committees of Joint Consultations, p. 15.

shows that the attendance at lower level of BHEL is slightly more than that of TISCO. But it is more in TISCO than in BHEL in case of middle and top levels. TISCO stands first even in case of overall attendance. However, it is not much ahead of BHEL. The overall picture shows that the rate of absenteeism is around 23 per cent in both the organizations. This rate of absenteeism hinders the interest of the members in deliberations.

Table 3.23 : Percentage Attendance of members at the Meetings for the year 1988–89

Level of the Council	BHEL	TISCO
Grass–root Level	77.75	76.59
Middle Level	73.25	74.37
Apex Level	79.49	81.13
Average Percengage of Attendance	**76.83**	**77.36**

Source : Compiled from the minutes of participative councils' meetings from BHEL and TISCO.

Hence, an enquiry was made to find out the reasons for the irregular attendance of the members (Table 3.24).

It is observed from the table that more than half of the members from BHEL expressed that fear of loss of production targets and personal problems are the reasons for irregular attendance at the meetings. Similarly, nearly forty per cent of the members from TISCO stated that loss of production target is one of the reasons for irregular attendance of members at the meetings.

As far as the shop council of BHEL is concerned the majority of the management representatives (37.50 per cent) opined that due to personal reasons, they were irregular in attending the meetings. Contrary to this, most of the workers' representatives (33.33 per cent) expressed that because of the heavy production schedules, they were not attending meetings regularly. A similar reason was expressed by the management representatives (58.51 per cent) in TISCO for their irregular attendance. But the workers' representatives (40.42 per cent) of TISCO expressed that personal problems were the reason for not attending the meetings regularly. Besides these reasons, a few members expressed that absence of information about the meetings schedule, showing protest against management, loss of over time, lack of faith in the implementation of decisions etc., were the reasons for irregular attendance.

Table 3.24 : Reasons for Irregular Attendance of Members

(Members responses are indicated in percentage)

Reason	BHEL						TISCO					
	Shop Council		*Joint Council*		*Joint Committee*		*Joint Departmental Council*		*Joint Works Council*		*Joint Consultative Council of Management*	
	M.R. N=24	W.R. N=24	M.R. N=4	W.R. N=4	M.R. N=2	W.R. N=2	M.R. N=94	W.R. N=94	M.R. N=2	W.R. N=2	M.R. N=2	W.R. N=2
No information about meeting schedule	--	16.67	--	50.00	--	--	--	--	--	--	--	--
Personal Reasons	37.50	8.33	100.00	--	100.00	100.00	24.47	40.42	100.00	100.00	100.00	100.00
As a mark of protest	--	8.33	--	--	--	--	--	4.26	--	--	--	--
No Faith in the implementation of decisions	12.50	16.67	--	--	--	--	--	4.26	--	--	--	--
Loss of overtime	--	16.67	--	--	--	--	--	--	--	--	--	--
Loss of Production targets	25.00	33.33	--	50.00	--	--	58.81	27.66	--	--	--	--
Others	25.00	--	--	--	--	--	17.02	23.40	--	--	--	--
Total	**100.00**	**100.00**	**100.00**	**100.00**	**100.00**	**100.00**	**100.00**	**100.00**	**100.00**	**100.00**	**100.00**	**100.00**

M.R. : Management Representatives; W.R. : Workers' Representatives **Source** : Data is collected through questionnaire.

All the management representatives in BHEL joint council stated that they could not attend the meetings due to their personal problems. But the workers' representatives stated that loss of production and absence of information about the meeting schedule were the reasons for their irregular attendance. The two types of representatives from TISCO's JWC stated that personal problems was the reason for not attending the meetings regularly. Similar reason was stated by both the representatives at apex level of both the organizations.

It is clear from the table 3.24 that the important reasons for irregular attendance were absence of information about meeting schedule, absence of faith in implementation of decisions, loss of overtime and loss of production targets. Absence of information and loss of production targets are due to lapses in the structure of the participative management schemes. Thus, the absenteeism is mostly due to the irregularities in the structure and working of participative management schemes. Hence, it is suggested that the structure should be modified in such a way that it does not affect the production target and the over time allowance of the workers. Further, the management has to take steps to make it work perfectly which in turn reduces the absenteeism due to the causes like the absence of information about meetings schedule.

4. Items Discussed

Supply of Information

Members of the various councils are generally supplied with adequate information on each issue of the agenda in the form of explanation or note to the agenda. This piece of information gives a clear and detailed picture of the history, alternatives and consequences etc., about the issues to the worker and management representatives. Both the parties face the problems if adequate information is not provided. Thus, it helps both the parties to discuss the issues from higher planes, minimize possible conflict, for understanding and to conduct the proceedings smoothly and effectively.

An attempt was made to find out whether adequate information is provided to the members or not. The opinions of both the parties are tabulated and presented in Table 3.25.

It is clear from this table that adequate information on each issue which are included in the agenda was frequently supplied as stated by only 46.67 per cent members from BHEL and 52.04 per cent members from TISCO. The number is more in TISCO than in BHEL. In both the

Table 3.25 : Supply of Adequate Information of Each Issue

(Members responses are indicated in percentage)

Frequency	BHEL						TISCO					
	Shop Council		*Joint Council*		*Joint Committee*		*Joint Depart-mental Council*		*Joint Works Council*		*Joint Consul-tative Council of Management*	
	M.R. N=24	W.R. N=24	M.R. N=4	W.R. N=4	M.R. N=2	W.R. N=2	M.R. N=94	W.R. N=94	M.R. N=2	W.R. N=2	M.R. N=2	W.R. N=2
Adequate information at all times	70.83	16.67	75.00	25.00	100.00	50.00	69.15	34.04	100.00	--	100.00	50.00
Adequate information at sometimes	8.33	16.67	25.00	75.00	--	50.00	7.45	25.53	--	100.00	--	50.00
No information	20.84	66.66	--	--	--	--	23.40	40.43	--	--	--	--
Total	**100.00**	**100.00**	**100.00**	**100.00**	**100.00**	**100.00**	**100.00**	**100.00**	**100.00**	**100.00**	**100.00**	**100.00**

M.R. : Management Representatives; W.R. : Workers' Representatives **Source** : Data is collected through questionnaire.

organizations most of the management representatives expressed that the information on the issues was frequently supplied. The percentage of number of members who expressed that no information was supplied on each issue to total is more in BHEL (35.00 per cent) than in TISCO (30.00 per cent).

The majority of the management representatives (70. 83 per cent) from BHEL shop council opined that adequate information on each issue is supplied to them at all times. Contrary to this, the workers' representatives (66.67 per cent) expressed that the information is not at all supplied to them. In TISCO 69.15 per cent of the management representatives stated that they received adequate information regularly. But most of the workers' representatives by stating that no information is supplied on the issues. Few members also opined that adequate information is supplied on the issues irregularly.

As far as joint council of BHEL is concerned, three–fourths of the management representatives stated that adequate information is supplied to them regularly, whereas same number of the workers' representatives stated that the information is supplied to them during some times only. In TISCO cent per cent of the management representatives opined that adequate information is supplied regularly. The information on the issues to be discussed in the meetings is supplied sometimes only as disclosed by cent per cent workers representatives from TISCO.

At the apex level all the management representatives from both organizations opined that the information is given regularly, whereas half of the workers' representatives from both the organizations differed with them by saying that the information is supplied some times only.

It is clear from the above table that the worker representatives from grass–root level in both the organizations felt that the adequate information is not supplied to them regularly and supplied but irregularly. At the middle and apex levels the case is a little better than the shop council. Hence, it is suggested that the chairman of the council should ensure supply of adequate information on all the items of the meetings.

Nature of Items Discussed

Participative management council take up and discuss various items based on their significance, their necessity on the scope of the council. Table 3.26 shows the nature–wise items discussed at all levels from their inception upto the end of March, 1988.

Table 3.26 : Nature of Items Discussed from the Date of Inception Till 31.3.1988

Items	BHEL		TISCO		Total	
	Number	*Per cent*	*Number*	*Per cent*	*Number*	*Per cent*
Production and Productivity	1,943	46.26	16,623	43.15	18,566	43.46
Safety	893	21.26	8.529	22.14	9,422	22.05
Welfare	947	22.55	2,797	7.26	3,744	8.76
Absenteeism	195	4.64	9,642	25.03	9,836	23.03
Personnel	222	5.29	933	2.42	1,155	2.70
Total	**4,200**	**100.00**	**38,524**	**100.00**	**42,724**	**100.00**

Source : Compiled from the minutes of Participative Council's Meetings from BHEL and TISCO.

It is observed from the table that 4,200 items were discussed in BHEL, while 38,524 were discussed in TISCO. In both the organizations the main emphasis has been given to production and productivity by discussing 1,943 (46.26 per cent) issues in BHEL and 16,623 issues (43.15 per cent) in TISCO. The issues relating to welfare were discussed mostly (22.55 per cent) next to production in BHEL whereas issues relating to absenteeism (25.03 per cent) were discussed next to production in TISCO. The members from both the organizations also discussed other items relating to safety and personal items.

The above analysis shows that issues relating to production and productivity and safety were discussed extensively in both the organizations. The issues relating to absenteeism were discussed extensively in TISCO whereas issues on welfare were discussed extensively in BHEL. It is observed that absenteeism is a crucial problem in TISCO, while welfare facilities are paid much attention in BHEL compared to that in TISCO.

Items of Production

The members were asked to identify the issues related to production, discussed in the participative councils. The analysis is presented in Table 3.27.

It is observed from the table that the majority of the management

Table 3.27 : Nature of Issues Discussed in Production Area

(Members responses are indicated in percentage)

Nature of Issues	BHEL						TISCO					
	Shop Council		*Joint Council*		*Joint Committee*		*Joint Departmental Council*		*Joint Works Council*		*Joint Consultative Council of Management*	
	M.R. N=24	W.R. N=24	M.R. N=4	W.R. N=4	M.R. N=2	W.R. N=2	M.R. N=94	W.R. N=94	M.R. N=2	W.R. N=2	M.R. N=2	W.R. N=2
Production policy	8.33	8.33	25.00	--	--	--	14.89	21.28	--	--	--	--
Regulating piece work	12.50	8.33	--	25.00	--	--	13.83	19.15	--	--	--	--
Determination of norms of productivity per unit/man/machine	25.00	29.17	25.00	25.00	--	100.00	18.09	9.57	50.00	--	50.00	--
Quality improvement of output	12.50	20.83	50.00	50.00	100.00	--	18.09	14.89	50.00	50.00	50.00	50.00
Optimum utilization of tools	16.67	12.50	--	--	--	--	14.89	19.15	--	50.00	--	50.00
Determination of sequence of work	12.50	12.50	--	--	--	--	11.70	8.51	--	--	--	--
Coordinating one's work	12.50	8.34	--	--	--	--	8.51	7.45	--	--	--	--
Total	**100.00**	**100.00**	**100.00**	**100.00**	**100.00**	**100.00**	**100.00**	**100.00**	**100.00**	**100.00**	**100.00**	**100.00**

M.R. : Management Representatives; W.R. : Workers' Representatives. **Source** : Data is collected through questionnaire.

(25.00 per cent) and worker representatives (29.17 per cent) expressed that the item of determination of norms of productivity per unit/man/machine was discussed frequently in the shop council of BHEL. Quality improvement of output is placed next in the discussions as stated by the members (12.50 per cent of management and 20.83 per cent of worker) from BHEL. The members of both the categories (18.09 per cent) in JDC of TISCO opined that the items they frequently discussed related to production policy. The other items discussed by the members are, optimum utilization of tools, determination of sequence of work, co–ordinating one's work etc. Thus it is clear that at the shop council, the members from both the organizations have discussed a wide range of items on various aspects relating to production.

At the middle level in BHEL, half of the management representatives and worker representatives opined that major issues discussed by them are related to quality improvement of output. The remaining members expressed that they discussed items relating to production policy, regulating piece work, determination of norms of productivity per unit/man/machine. Most of the members (50.00 per cent) from TISCO also expressed a similar opinion.

At the top level, the members from both the organizations have discussed the items like determination of norms of productivity, quality improvement of output and optimum utilization of tools.

The above analysis shows that items like improvement of quality and determination of norms of productivity were discussed at middle level of both the organizations. All the issues in production including production policy were not discussed at apex level in BHEL and both at apex level and middle level in TISCO. This major lacuna should be corrected by the management at the top level.

Items of Personnel

Though there are various forums like grievance procedure, collective bargaining etc., to solve the worker's problem, they are also normally discussed in various councils of the participative management as they are included in the items to be discussed in the participative management schemes. Table 3.28 shows the nature of worker problems discussed in the area of personnel. The members responded to more than one issue.

The majority of the members (52.08 per cent) from BHEL opined that they discussed mostly the items relating to working conditions. More than fifty per cent of the workers' representatives from BHEL stated that

Table 3.28 : Nature of Issues Discussed in Personnel Area

(Members responses are indicated in percentage)

Nature of Issues	BHEL						TISCO					
	Shop Council		*Joint Council*		*Joint Committee*		*Joint Depart-mental Council*		*Joint Works Council*		*Joint Consul-tative Council of Management*	
	M.R. N=24	W.R. N=24	M.R. N=4	W.R. N=4	M.R. N=2	W.R. N=2	M.R. N=94	W.R. N=94	M.R. N=2	W.R. N=2	M.R. N=2	W.R. N=2
Working conditions	50.00	54.17	75.00	50.00	50.00	50.00	65.96	64.89	50.00	100.00	50.00	50.00
Training and develop-ment	25.00	25.00	100.00	50.00	100.00	100.00	40.43	34.04	100.00	50.00	100.00	50.00
Work Allocations	20.83	12.50	25.00	100.00	50.00	50.00	36.17	45.74	100.00	50.00	50.00	100.00
Holiday rosters	12.50	20.83	50.00	100.00	100.00	50.00	28.72	37.23	100.00	50.00	100.00	100.00
Overtime	12.50	33.33	--	75.00	--	--	--	--	--	--	--	--
Welfare	33.33	50.00	75.00	100.00	50.00	50.00	67.02	74.47	100.00	100.00	50.00	100.00
Housing	12.50	39.83	50.00	75.00	50.00	100.00	68.08	72.34	50.00	50.00	50.00	100.00
Rewards & Prizes	20.83	58.33	100.00	100.00	100.00	50.00	71.28	73.40	100.00	50.00	100.00	100.00
Absenteeism	25.00	37.50	100.00	25.00	50.00	50.00	79.79	74.47	100.00	50.00	50.00	50.00
Shift System	12.50	58.33	--	50.00	50.00	50.00	51.06	44.68	--	50.00	--	--

M.R. : Management Representatives; W.R. : Workers' Representatives. **Source** : Data is collected through questionnaire.

the items discussed in the shop council are welfare, rewards and prizes, shift system etc. The remaining members from BHEL's shop council stated that they discussed issues like training and development, work allocation, holiday rosters, overtime, housing and absenteeism. The majority of the JDC members of TISCO opined that the issues discussed by them related to working conditions (65.42 per cent), welfare (70.75 per cent) and absenteeism (77.13 per cent). The remaining members expressed that they discussed items relating to training and development, work allocations, holiday rosters and shift system.

At the joint council in BHEL, more than three–fourths of management representatives discussed issues relating to working conditions, training and development, welfare, rewards, prizes and absenteeism. In addition to these issues, most of the workers' representatives discussed work allocations, holiday rosters, overtime, housing, shift system. Almost the same opinion was expressed by the JWC members of TISCO.

At the apex level of both the organizations, all the items relating to personnel were discussed.

Council-wise analysis shows that items like, training and development, work allocations, rewards and prizes etc., were discussed mostly in middle and apex level councils, whereas other items were discussed at the grass–root level.

The members mostly (53.33 per cent) discussed items relating to working conditions in BHEL whereas items relating to absenteeism were discussed by majority (76.53 per cent) of members in TISCO.

The analysis shows that some of the issues like housing, working conditions, which otherwise could have been solved by the other forums, were also discussed in the participative councils. Hence, it is suggested that the management should take steps to discuss the personnel issues mostly through grievance procedure collective bargaining and other forums rather than referring those issues to the participative management.

5. Participation Nature and Extent

Environment in Meetings

A conducive psychological and social environment in addition to physical environment plays a significant role in the successful conduct of the meetings, as it provides scope for interaction and communication with one another freely. It also influence the nature of members' participation in meetings. The members were asked to express their experience regarding the environment of the meetings (Table 3.29).

Table 3.29 : Nature of Environment in Meeting Place

(Members responses are indicated in percentage)

Environment	BHEL						TISCO					
	Shop Council		*Joint Council*		*Joint Committee*		*Joint Depart-mental Council*		*Joint Works Council*		*Joint Consul-tative Council of Management*	
	M.R. N=24	W.R. N=24	M.R. N=4	W.R. N=4	M.R. N=2	W.R. N=2	M.R. N=94	W.R. N=94	M.R. N=2	W.R. N=2	M.R. N=2	W.R. N=2
Congenial	100.00	91.66	100.00	75.00	100.00	100.00	100.00	100.00	100.00	100.00	100.00	100.00
Uncongenial	--	--	--	--	--	--	--	--	--	--	--	--
Partly congenial	--	4.17	--	25.00	--	--	--	--	--	--	--	--
Can't say	--	4.17	--	--	--	--	--	--	--	--	--	--
Total	**100.00**	**100.00**	**100.00**	**100.00**	**100.00**	**100.00**	**100.00**	**100.00**	**100.00**	**100.00**	**100.00**	**100.00**

M.R. : Management Representatives; W.R. : Workers' Representatives **Source** : Data is collected through questionnaire.

It is observed from the table that cent per cent of the management representatives and more than 90 per cent of workers' representatives from BHEL shop council expressed that they experienced a congenial environment in the meeting place. An insignificant number of workers' representatives from BHEL shop council stated that the environment in meetings is congenial some times only. All the members from TISCO's JDC stated that a congenial environment existed in the meetings.

As far as the middle level and apex levels are concerned, all the members expressed that there is a congenial environment at the meetings.

The above analysis shows that almost all the members experienced a congenial environment at the meetings. This might have resulted in free flow of communication and active involvement of members. This would naturally contribute to the co–operative nature of participation of the members in the meetings.

Nature of Participation in Meetings

Table 3.30 shows the nature of members' participation in meetings. It is observed from the table that fifty per cent of the management representatives from BHEL shop council felt that the participation at the meetings is co–operative. It is interesting to note that a higher number (58.00 per cent) of workers' representatives experienced co–operative nature of participation. Contrary to this, the majority of management representatives (53.19 per cent) from TISCO stated that the participation in meetings is reasonably good. Participation in the meetings is co–operative as perceived by half of the workers' representatives. Equal number of management and workers' representatives (29.17 per cent) from BHEL shop council opined that the participation in the meetings are reasonably good. More than one–third of the management and workers' representatives felt that the participation in the meetings is co-operative and reasonably good respectively. It is also interesting to observe that more management representatives (20.83 per cent) than the workers' representatives (12.50 per cent) in BHEL stated that the participation in the meetings is indifferent. The case is vice versa in TISCO.

As far as the joint council in BHEL is concerned, half of the management representatives expressed that the members' participation at the meetings is indifferent. Disagreeing with this opinion fifty per cent of the workers' representative from BHEL felt that the participation at the meetings is reasonably good. Participation in the meetings is reasonably good as reported by cent per cent of management representatives and

Table 3.30 : Nature of Member Participation in Meeting

(*Members responses are indicated in percentage*)

Nature	BHEL						TISCO					
	Shop Council		*Joint Council*		*Joint Committee*		*Joint Depart-mental Council*		*Joint Works Council*		*Joint Consul-tative Council of Management*	
	M.R. N=24	W.R. N=24	M.R. N=4	W.R. N=4	M.R. N=2	W.R. N=2	M.R. N=94	W.R. N=94	M.R. N=2	W.R. N=2	M.R. N=2	W.R. N=2
Fully co-operative	50.00	58.33	25.00	25.00	50.00	50.00	37.23	50.00	--	50.00	50.00	--
Reasonably cooperative	29.17	29.17	25.00	50.00	50.00	50.00	53.19	39.36	100.00	50.00	50.00	100.00
Indifferent	20.83	12.50	50.00	25.00	--	--	9.58	10.64	--	--	--	--
Total	**100.00**	**100.00**	**100.00**	**100.00**	**100.00**	**100.00**	**100.00**	**100.00**	**100.00**	**100.00**	**100.00**	**100.00**

M.R. : Management Representatives; W.R. : Workers' Representatives. **Source** : Data is collected through questionnaire.

50.00 per cent of the workers' representatives from TISCO's JWC. The participation in the meetings is co–operative and reasonably good, as stated by an equal number of management and worker representatives from BHEL.

The members' participation at the meetings is reasonably good and co–operative, as expressed by an equal number of management and workers' representatives from BHEL and TISCO at the top level council. Contrary to this, cent per cent worker representatives from TISCO's JCCM expressed that the participation of the members in the councils is reasonably good.

It is further observed from the table that there is difference of opinion among the members of the three councils. At the grass–root level, the majority of the members (45.76 per cent) opined that the participation in the meetings are co–operative, whereas at middle and apex levels, the members' participation is reasonable good.

The members' participation in the meetings is co-operative in BHEL than in TISCO as opined by the members. Also the number of members who expressed that the participation is indifferent in meetings is more in BHEL (21.66 per cent) than in TISCO (9.69 per cent).

The above analysis shows that majority of the members viewed that the other members co–operated with them in the proceedings of the meetings. However, some members' participation was indifferent. An analysis of reasons for indifferent participation necessary before offering suggestions for co-operative participation.

Reasons for indifferent participation in meetings are presented in Table 3.31.

The Majority of the management (60.00 per cent) and workers' representatives (66.67 per cent) from BHEL shop council perceived that lack of interest in the committee is the reason for indifferent participation. The same opinion was expressed by the members of TISCO's JDC. Nearly one–fourth of the members from both the organizations stated that the present duration of the meeting is one of the reasons for indifferent participation of the members in the meetings. The remaining members expressed that the reason for their indifferent participation is 'lack of confidence in other'.

At the joint council in BHEL, the members explained the important reasons for indifferent participation in the meetings are lack of interest in the committee and lack of confidence in others.

Table 3.31 : Reasons for Indifference of Members in the Meetings

(Members responses are indicated in percentage)

Opinion	BHEL						TISCO					
	Shop Council		*Joint Council*		*Joint Committee*		*Joint Departmental Council*		*Joint Works Council*		*Joint Consultative Council of Management*	
	M.R. N=5	W.R. N=3	M.R. N=2	W.R. N=1	M.R.	W.R.	M.R. N=9	W.R. N=10	M.R.	W.R.	M.R.	W.R.
Lack of interest in the committee	60.00	66.67	50.00	100.00	--	--	44.44	40.00	--	--	--	--
Lack of confidence in others	20.00	--	50.00	--	--	--	44.44	20.00	--	--	--	--
Insufficient duration of the meeting	20.00	33.33	--	--	--	--	11.12	40.00	--	--	--	--
Total	**100.00**	**100.00**	**100.00**	**100.00**	**--**	**--**	**100.00**	**100.00**	**--**	**--**	**--**	**--**

M.R. : Management Representatives; W.R. : Workers' Representatives. **Source** : Data is collected through questionnaire.

It is, therefore, suggested that the management should create interest among members through educational programmes and also create confidence in other members through sensitivity training. Another reason was found to be insufficient duration of the meetings. The members during the interview expressed that the meetings should be conducted for atleast three to four hours. And an element of flexibility should also be provided in case of emergency.

Degree of Openness in the Discussions

The deliberations of the proceedings, the quality of interactions in the meetings and the quality of decisions are mostly influenced by the openness in discussions among members. Openness in discussions helps the members to understand one other completely and reduces interpersonal conflict. Against this background, an attempt is made to find out the degree of openness experienced by various members during the proceedings. Table 3.32 presents the analysis of the degree of openness in the discussions.

It is observed from the table that the majority of the management representatives (45.83 per cent) from BHEL shop council opined that the degree of openness in the meetings was between 41—60 per cent. Contrary to this the workers' representatives (37.50 per cent) opined that the degree of openness was between 61—80 per cent. Very few members (6.25 per cent) had expressed that the discussions were 81 to 100 per cent open. In TISCO's JDC majority of management (34.04 per cent) and workers' representatives (37.23 per cent) expressed the opinions that the degree of openness in the discussions were between 41—60 per cent and 61—80 per cent respectively. Only 16.00 per cent of the members from TISCO expressed that the discussions were 81—100 per cent open.

As far as the joint council in BHEL is concerned, fifty per cent of the management and workers' representatives, stated that the degree of openness in the discussion were between 61—80 per cent and 21—40 per cent respectively. Twenty five per cent of management and workers' representatives (each) stated that the degree of openness in the discussions was between 41—60 per cent. In the JWC of TISCO, fifty per cent of the management representatives and cent per cent of the workers' representatives perceived that the degree of openness in discussions was between 61—80 per cent.

As far as the top level is concerned, cent per cent of the management and worker representatives from BHEL stated that openness in the

Table 3.32 : Extent of Openness in Discussions

(Members responses are indicated in percentage)

Extent	BHEL						TISCO					
	Shop Council		*Joint Council*		*Joint Committee*		*Joint Depart-mental Council*		*Joint Works Council*		*Joint Consul-tative Council of Management*	
	M.R. N=24	W.R. N=24	M.R. N=4	W.R. N=4	M.R. N=2	W.R. N=2	M.R. N=94	W.R. N=94	M.R. N=2	W.R. N=2	M.R. N=2	W.R. N=2
Upto 20%	--	4.17	--	--	--	--	--	--	--	--	--	--
21–40%	12.50	20.83	25.00	50.00	--	--	11.71	12.77	--	--	--	--
41–60%	45.84	33.33	25.00	25.00	--	--	34.04	37.23	50.00	--	--	100.00
61–80%	33.33	37.50	50.00	25.00	100.00	100.00	34.04	37.23	50.00	100.00	100.00	--
81–100%	8.33	4.17	--	--	--	--	20.21	12.77	--	--	--	--
Total	**100.00**	**100.00**	**100.00**	**100.00**	**100.00**	**100.00**	**100.00**	**100.00**	**100.00**	**100.00**	**100.00**	**100.00**

M.R. : Management Representatives; W.R. : Workers' Representatives. **Source** : Data is collected through questionnaire.

discussions was between 61—80 per cent. Contrary to this, there is difference of opinion among management and workers' representatives in TISCO as the management representatives expressed that openness in the discussions was between 61—80 per cent and the workers representatives felt that it was between 41—60 per cent.

It is further observed from the table that at the lower level, the degree of openness in the meetings was only between 41—60 per cent, whereas at the middle and apex levels it was between 61—80 per cent. Organization–wise analysis shows that there is almost common opinion among the members in both the organizations. But some members of BHEL expressed that the degree of openness in the discussions was less than 40.00 per cent.

It is clear from the above analysis that the majority of the management representatives at the shop council experienced the openness up to 60.00 per cent in BHEL and up to 80.00 per cent in TISCO whereas the workers' representatives experienced upto 80.00 per cent in BHEL and TISCO. Therefore, the management of BHEL has to create an awareness among members about the significance of openness through various training programmes.

Domination in the Discussions

A less degree of openness generally leads to discussions being dominated by some members of either of the group. An attempt was made to find out the nature of domination in the discussions. Table 3.33 shows the domination in the discussions.

Nearly four-fifths of the management representatives from BHEL shop council opined that most the discussions were dominated by the workers. Contrary to this, the management representatives dominated the meetings as stated by more than two-thirds of workers' representatives. More than four-fifths of the management representatives at the JDC of TISCO perceived that the meetings are dominated by the workers' representatives. Contrary to this, discussions are dominated by the management members as opined by four-fifths of the workers' representatives.

At middle level, fifty per cent of the management representatives from BHEL felt that the discussions were dominated by the workers. Whereas cent per cent of the workers' representatives expressed the vice-versa. Cent per cent of the management representatives of TISCO has expressed that they do not have any idea regarding the domination in the

Table 3.33 : Members Domination in the Discussions

(Members responses are indicated in percentage)

Opinion	BHEL						TISCO					
	Shop Council		*Joint Council*		*Joint Committee*		*Joint Depart-mental Council*		*Joint Works Council*		*Joint Consul-tative Council of Management*	
	M.R. N=24	W.R. N=24	M.R. N=4	W.R. N=4	M.R. N=2	W.R. N=2	M.R. N=94	W.R. N=94	M.R. N=2	W.R. N=2	M.R. N=2	W.R. N=2
Dominated by manage-ment representatives	4.17	70.84	--	100.00	--	50.00	--	79.79	--	100.00	--	--
Dominated by workers representatives	79.17	8.33	50.00	--	--	--	84.04	2.13	--	--	--	--
No idea	16.66	20.83	50.00	--	100.00	50.00	15.96	18.08	100.00	--	100.00	100.00
Total	**100.00**	**100.00**	**100.00**	**100.00**	**100.00**	**10.00**	**100.00**	**100.00**	**100.00**	**100.00**	**100.00**	**100.00**

M.R. : Management Representatives; W.R. : Workers' Representatives. **Source** : Data is collected through questionnaire.

meetings. All the workers' representatives stated that the meetings are dominated by the management representatives.

At the apex level also, one workers' representative from BHEL expressed that the meetings were dominated by the management representatives. The remaining members from both the organizations stated that they do not have any idea regarding this matter.

There are contradictory opinions among the management and workers' representatives at all levels in both the organizations.

The above analysis shows that both the parties accused each other regarding the domination, which shows less degree of openness in the discussions. Table 3.32 shows the degree of openness between 40—60 per cent as experienced by majority of the members. Hence it is suggested that the members of both groups give up the practice of domination and co-operate in developing free and frank environment during meetings.

Hurdles in the Effectiveness of Participation

There may be a number of hurdles which prevent or hamper the conducive environment in addition to the absence of openness in the participative management. Hurdles in the effectiveness of participation as expressed by the members, are presented in Table 3.34. Lack of proper legislative frame work is one of hurdles for effectiveness of the participation as expressed by 45.83 per cent of the management representatives from BHEL shop council. Limitations of management and unions in giving their free and frank opinion are a hurdle in the way of effectiveness of participation as expressed by two-thirds of the workers' representatives of BHEL. The other hurdles against effectiveness of participation as explained by the members of BHEL are the bureaucratic attitude of management, lack of mutual trust and confidence between the representatives. The hurdle for effectiveness of participative management is lack of mutual trust and confidence between the representatives as expressed by the management representatives (45.74 per cent) from TISCO. More number of workers' representatives (51.06 per cent) have also expressed the same opinion. The management (42.55 per cent) and workers' representatives (51.06 per cent) from TISCO's JDC also opined that the limitations of management and unions to give out their free and frank opinion is one of the hurdle for effectiveness of the participative management. Some members also expressed that bureaucratic attitude of the management is one of the hurdle.

Table 3.34 : Hurdles in the Effective Functioning of Participative Management Schemes

(Members responses are indicated in percentage)

Hurdles	BHEL						TISCO					
	Shop Council		*Joint Council*		*Joint Committee*		*Joint Departmental Council*		*Joint Works Council*		*Joint Consultative Council of Management*	
	M.R. N=24	W.R. N=24	M.R. N=4	W.R. N=4	M.R. N=2	W.R. N=2	M.R. N=94	W.R. N=94	M.R. N=2	W.R. N=2	M.R. N=2	W.R. N=2
Lack of mutual trust and confidence between the representatives	25.00	25.00	25.00	50.00	50.00	50.00	45.74	51.06	--	100.00	--	--
Bureaucratic attitude of Management	8.33	50.00	--	75.00	--	100.00	20.21	43.62	--	--	--	--
Limitations of Management, unions to give out their free and frank opinion	33.33	66.67	75.00	50.00	100.00	50.00	42.55	51.06	100.00	100.00	100.00	--
Lack of proper legislative framework	45.83	29.17	50.00	50.00	100.00	100.00	--	--	--	--	--	--

M.R. : Management Representatives; W.R. : Workers' Representatives **Source** : Data is collected through questionnaire.
Totals do not tally as each member expressed more than one opinion.

Three-fourths of the management representatives and same number of the workers' representatives from BHEL joint council stated that the main hurdles are absence of free and frank opinion by the management and union, and the bureaucratic attitude of the management respectively. In TISCO's JWC also the members opined the same. Some members from BHEL also expressed that the hurdles are lack of proper legislative framework and lack of mutual trust and confidence between the representatives.

At the apex level, all the members (100.00 per cent) from BHEL expressed that the absence of proper legislative frame work is one of the hurdle for effective participation. But in TISCO, cent per cent of the members stated that absence of free and frank opinion is the main hurdle for effective participation of members in the meetings.

The majority of the members at grass-root level (47.06 per cent) expressed that the management and unions to give out free and frank opinion as the hurdle. The same reason was expressed by the majority of the members from middle and apex level members.

Table 3.34 shows that the majority of the members feel that management and unions are not free and open in expressing their opinions. Lack of proper understanding, rival attitude, win-lose policy might be the reasons for the absence of free and openness of both the parties. Hence, it is suggested that the management should take an active part in discussing the issues openly with the trade union leaders and making the trade union also to be open. Members also expressed that absence of mutual trust and confidence between the representatives. The another reason for ineffective participation is the bureaucratic attitude of the management. Bureaucratic and participative systems cannot go hand in hand. When management choose the participative system, it should not rely upon the bureaucratic system of management. Some representatives view that absence of proper legislative frame work is a hurdle in this process.

The organization structure and culture should provide a completely free and positive environment to make the discussions and proceedings of the participative management effective.

6. Decisions Made

A decision is the selection of a course of action. It is a choice from among a set of alternatives. According to Felix M. Lopez, "a decision represents judgement; a final resolution of a conflict of needs, means or goals, and a commitment to action made in the fact of uncertainty complexity and even irrationality[1]." In participative forums, the decisions play an important role. The outcome of the discussions lies in the decisions.

After a thorough and in-depth discussion of each item, the members at each meeting make decisions. The various types of making decisions in the meeting are voting, consensus, accepting chairman's opinion and through the force of the group. Here, an attempt is made to enquire into the method of arriving the decisions in the meetings based on the opinions. The opinions are presented in Table 3.35.

The majority of the management representatives (54.17 per cent) form BHEL's shop council opined that the method of arriving at decisions is only through consensus. Majority of the workers' representatives 41.67 per cent) also supported the same. Contrary to this most of the management representatives (67.02 per cent) from TISCO's JDC expressed that the voting method is used for decision-making in the meetings. But the workers' representatives (39.36 per cent) differed with the opinion of management by saying that decisions are taken in the meetings through consensus method. Some members from BHEL also expressed that for decision-making in the meetings, voting (33.33 per cent) was followed. In TISCO also, similar number of members expressed this opinion.

At the joint council in BHEL, three–fourths of the management representatives and workers' representatives state that to arrive at decisions in the meetings, the method of consensus and chairman's opinion respectively were relied upon, whereas in TISCO's JWC the members expressed that the method of arriving at the decisions are by voting, consensus and accepting the chairman's opinion.

The methods of arriving at decisions in the meetings are by voting and consensus, as opined by the management and workers' representatives at apex level from both the organizations.

It is further observed from the table that at the lower level, the members expressed that decisions are made by consensus, voting and by accepting the chairman's opinion, whereas at middle and apex levels the members opined that voting and consensus are the methods used for the decision-making.

---

1. Lpez, Felix, 'The Making of a Manager', Taraporewala, Bombay, 1977, p. 73.

Table 3.35 : Method of Arriving Decision in the Meetings

(Members responses are indicated in percentage)

Opinion	BHEL						TISCO					
	Shop Council		*Joint Council*		*Joint Committee*		*Joint Departmental Council*		*Joint Works Council*		*Joint Consultative Council of Management*	
	M.R. N=24	W.R. N=24	M.R. N=4	W.R. N=4	M.R. N=2	W.R. N=2	M.R. N=94	W.R. N=94	M.R. N=2	W.R. N=2	M.R. N=2	W.R. N=2
Voting	33.33	33.33	25.00	--	50.00	50.00	67.02	38.30	50.00	--	50.00	50.00
Consensus	54.17	41.67	75.00	25.00	50.00	50.00	20.21	39.36	50.00	50.00	50.00	50.00
Accepting the Chairman's opinion	12.50	16.67	--	75.00	--	--	12.78	22.34	--	50.00	--	--
Force of the group	--	8.33	--	--	--	--	--	--	--	--	--	--
Total	**100.00**	**100.00**	**100.00**	**100.00**	**100.00**	**10.00**	**100.00**	**100.00**	**100.00**	**100.00**	**100.00**	**100.00**

M.R. : Management Representatives; W.R. : Workers' Representatives. **Source** : Data is collected through questionnaire.

It is viewed from the above analysis that majority of the members from all levels expressed that they arrived at decisions through consensus. Next highest number of members viewed that they arrived at decisions by voting. However, there are incidents of accepting the chairman's opinions and accepting the decision of the group by force. It is suggested that the chairman and groups should avoid such type of practices altogether. It is also suggested that the chairman has to create such an environment for making the decisions by consensus rather than by voting or by any other method.

Justification of the Decisions

Though decisions are made by consensus, sometimes, they are thrust on members owing to the force of the chairman or some groups. Hence, the justification of the decisions made may be doubtful. Members were asked to express their view regarding the justification of the decisions made (Table 3.36).

It is observed from the table that two-thirds of the management representatives and 54.16 per cent of the workers' representatives from BHEL's shop council expressed that the decisions are taken on the basis of the merit of the case at the meetings. Similarly, more than 80.00 per cent of management and workers' representatives each from TISCO's joint departmental council stated that the decisions are taken at the meetings on the basis of the merit of the case. Some members from BHEL (27.08 per cent) and TISCO (14.89 per cent) also stated that the decisions taken at the meetings are partly biased. Few members from BHEL's shop council perceived that the decisions taken at the meetings are fully biased.

At the middle level, all the management representatives from both the organizations stated that decisions are taken on the basis of the merit of the case whereas three-fourths of the workers' members from BHEL and half of the worker representatives from TISCO opined that the decisions are taken at the meeting are partly biased.

All the members at the top level in both the organizations felt that decisions are made on the basis of the merit of the case. At the grass-root level, some members felt that the decisions are biased fully/partly. But at the middle and apex levels except some all the members expressed that the decisions are taken on the basis of the merit of the issue.

In between the two organizations, majority of the decisions in TISCO are taken on the basis of merit of the case.

Table 3.36 : Justification of Decision at the Meetings

(Members responses are indicated in percentage)

Justification	BHEL						TISCO					
	Shop Council		*Joint Council*		*Joint Committee*		*Joint Depart-mental Council*		*Joint Works Council*		*Joint Consul-tative Council of Management*	
	M.R. N=24	W.R. N=24	M.R. N=4	W.R. N=4	M.R. N=2	W.R. N=2	M.R. N=94	W.R. N=94	M.R. N=2	W.R. N=2	M.R. N=2	W.R. N=2
Merit of the case	66.67	54.16	100.00	75.00	100.00	100.00	88.30	81.92	100.00	50.00	100.00	100.00
Fully biased	8.33	16.67	--	--	--	--	--	--	--	--	--	--
Partly biased	25.00	29.17	--	25.00	--	--	11.70	18.08	--	50.00	--	--
Total	**100.00**	**100.00**	**100.00**	**100.00**	**100.00**	**100.00**	**100.00**	**100.00**	**100.00**	**100.00**	**100.00**	**100.00**

M.R. : Management Representatives; W.R. : Workers' Representatives. **Source** : Data is collected through questionnaire.

Though the majority of the members expressed that the decisions are made based on merit, some of the members expressed that the decisions are either fully or partially biased. This is due to the influence of the chairman or some groups. Hence, it is suggested that there should not be any force in making decisions. Otherwise, the entire effort of participative management will be an exercise in futility.

7. Supply of Minutes

The secretary of the council prepares the minutes after the meetings are over and gets them approved by the chairman. The approved minutes should be circulated regularly to all the members without fail. But some times, either because of irregularity or due to the negligence of the secretary of the council, the minutes may not be supplied to the members in time. Table 3.37 shows the regularity of supply of minutes to the members.

The minutes are supplied regularly in time, as opined by two-thirds of the management representatives and just over fifty per cent of the workers' representatives from BHEL's shop council. Some members also expressed the non-receipt of the minutes supply of the minutes now and then. In TISCO's JDC 80.00 per cent of the management and nearly 50.00 per cent of the workers' representatives stated that they are in receipt of the minutes regularly. Similarly 28.72 and 13.83 per cent of workers and management members from TISCO expressed that the minutes are supplied now and then and not at all provided respectively.

As far as the joint council in BHEL is concerned, three-fourths of the management and half of the workers' representatives are in receipt of minutes regularly. Few members also opined that the minutes are supplied now and then and not at all provided, whereas in TISCO the minutes are received by the members regularly, as stated by cent per cent of the management representatives and fifty per cent of the workers' representatives. The remaining workers' representatives expressed that the minutes are supplied now and then.

All the members belonging to both the categories from both the organizations at the apex councils felt that they received the minutes regularly.

At the grass-root level, nearly thirty-five per cent of the members complained that they never received the minutes and received minutes now and then only. Though there are complaints of this kind at middle and apex levels, the majority of the members are satisfied with the receipt of minutes in time.

Table 3.37 : Regularity in Supplying the Minutes of the Meetings

(Members responses are indicated in percentage)

Regularity in Supply	BHEL						TISCO					
	Shop Council		*Joint Council*		*Joint Committee*		*Joint Departmental Council*		*Joint Works Council*		*Joint Consultative Council of Management*	
	M.R. N=24	W.R. N=24	M.R. N=4	W.R. N=4	M.R. N=2	W.R. N=2	M.R. N=94	W.R. N=94	M.R. N=2	W.R. N=2	M.R. N=2	W.R. N=2
Supplied regularly	66.67	54.17	75.00	50.00	100.00	100.00	80.85	53.19	100.00	50.00	100.00	100.00
Supplied now and then	25.00	33.33	25.00	25.00	--	--	13.83	28.72	--	50.00	--	--
Not at all provided	8.33	12.50	--	25.00	--	--	5.32	18.09	--	--	--	--
Total	**100.00**	**100.00**	**100.00**	**100.00**	**100.00**	**10.00**	**100.00**	**100.00**	**100.00**	**100.00**	**100.00**	**100.00**

M.R. : Management Representatives; W.R. : Workers' Representatives. **Source** : Data is collected through questionnaire.

The analysis shows that though the minutes are supplied regularly to some members, they are supplied now and then to some members and not at all to some members. It is suggested that the secretary of the council concerned should accept the responsibility of sending the minutes regularly.

8. Implementation of Decisions

It is always a complaint from the side of the workers that they have to pursue and force the management to implement the decisions. But the management says that they have to implement the decisions on their own. Hence, an enquiry is made to find out the position. Table 3.38 shows the parties who took the initiative to execute the decisions.

It is observed from the table that 54.17 per cent of management representatives from BHEL's shop council agreed that they implemented the decisions with the initiative of workers. As many as two-thirds of the workers' representatives from BHEL shop council expressed that they pursued the matter and force the management in execution of the decisions. In TISCO also, more than two-thirds of management and workers' representatives also expressed the same. The management took initiative in executing the decisions as expressed by 39.58 per cent of the members form BHEL and 19.68 per cent members form TISCO.

As far as middle level council is concerned, in BHEL all the management representatives stated that they took the initiative in executing the decisions, whereas fifty per cent of the workers' representatives expressed that they pursued and forced the management in executing the decisions. In TISCO also, all the management representatives and 50.00 per cent workers' representatives expressed the same opinions as perceived by the members of BHEL.

At the apex level, cent per cent of the management representatives and 50.00 per cent of the workers' representatives from both the organizations stated that the management took initiative in executing the decisions. Other workers' representatives expressed that they pursued and forced the management in execution of the decisions.

Most of the management representatives as well workers' representatives viewed that the decisions are implemented due to the initiative of the workers. It is therefore, suggested that management should take the initiative in implementing the decisions. This sustains interest among the workers in the utility of participative scheme.

Table 3.38 : Parties Who Took Initiative to Execute the Decisions

(Members responses are indicated in percentage)

Parties who took Initiative	BHEL						TISCO					
	Shop Council		*Joint Council*		*Joint Committee*		*Joint Departmental Council*		*Joint Works Council*		*Joint Consultative Council of Management*	
	M.R. N=24	W.R. N=24	M.R. N=4	W.R. N=4	M.R. N=2	W.R. N=2	M.R. N=94	W.R. N=94	M.R. N=2	W.R. N=2	M.R. N=2	W.R. N=2
Management	45.83	33.33	100.00	50.00	100.00	50.00	19.15	20.21	100.00	50.00	100.00	50.00
Management and workers	54.17	66.67	--	50.00	--	50.00	80.85	79.79	--	50.00	--	50.00
Total	**100.00**	**100.00**	**100.00**	**100.00**	**100.00**	**10.00**	**100.00**	**100.00**	**100.00**	**100.00**	**100.00**	**100.00**

M.R. : Management Representatives; W.R. : Workers' Representatives **Source** : Data is collected through questionnaire.

The management implements the decisions taken on a priority basis. However, implementation of the decisions in time is more important as it is the ultimate outcome of the entire process of participative management.

Table 3.39 shows the time taken to implement the decisions.

Table 3.39 : Time Taken to Implement the Decisions since Inception till 31.3.1988

Time Taken	BHEL		TISCO		Total	
	Number	*Per cent*	*Number*	*Per cent*	*Number*	*Per cent*
Less than 1 month	1,839	43.79	27,873	72.35	29,712	69.54
1–2 Months	234	5.57	190	0.49	424	0.99
2–3 Months	347	8.26	188	0.48	535	1.25
Above 3 Months	472	11.24	543	1.41	1,015	2.38
Decisions turned down or dropped	1,308	31.14	9,730	25.26	11,038	25.84
Total	**4,200**	**100.00**	**38,524**	**100.00**	**42,724**	**100.00**

Source : Compiled from the Minutes of Participative Councils Meetings from BHEL and TISCO.

The table explains that out of 4,200 decisions taken in the meetings up to 31-3-1988, 2,892 (68.86 per cent) decision were implemented in BHEL. The majority of the implemented decisions i.e., 1,838 (43.79 per cent) were implemented in less than one month. As many as 472 (11.24 per cent) decisions were implemented after three months of the meeting. As per the records of the organizations, the time taken to implement 8.26 per cent and 5.87 per cent of decisions were 2 to 3 months and 1 to 2 months respectively.

Out of 38,524 decisions taken in TISCO 28.794 (74.74 per cent) were implemented upto 31-3-1988. Among the decisions implemented, the majority of them i.e. 27,873 (72,35 per cent) were implemented in less than one month. The other decisions i.e. 921 (2.39 per cent) were implemented in 1 to 3 months.

The analysis shows that majority of the members expressed that the decisions were implemented within one month. But there are several instances of implementing the decisions after three months. This type of practice generally develops an indifferent attitude among the members, are an absence of trust in the chairman and the scheme in toto. Hence, it is suggested that the management should not take any chance of using delaying tactics in implementing the decisions. It is unfortunate that a significant number of decisions was turned down. This type of practice would invariably degenerate interest and confidence in the scheme. Hence, it is suggested that the management should not think of dropping the decisions.

Conclusion

The systematic structure and effective functioning of workers' participation in management contribute to sound industrial relations. It is observed from the above analysis that there are certain limitations in the organization structure. Hence, it is suggested that the participative management in both the organizations should be extended to board level in addition to creating an agenda sub–committee in all councils at all levels in BHEL. Further, the objectives and related functions regarding democratization at work place and human growth and dignity at work place should be incorporated in the objectives of participative management in both the organizations. It is suggested for rotation of chairmanship and co–chairmanship between the representatives of workers and management for complete democratization of participative management in BHEL as is the practice in TISCO.

Conducting of training programmes to the members and non–members in various aspects of participative management will further enhance the awareness and interest in participative management schemes.

Involvement of the members in the schemes of participative management should be effective only when they are encouraged and consulted to participate at each and every stage of the working. Hence, it is suggested that the members should be consulted even in the preparation of agenda. Circulation of agenda and notices in time is not perfect in both the organizations which may degenerate the interest of the members. Hence, it is suggested that complete care should be taken in this regard. The structure of the organization affected the members' attendance, nature of items discussed and extent of members' attendance, nature of items discussed and extent of members' participation. Hence, it is suggested to modify the existing organizational structure by avoiding duplication in functioning and incorporating the principles of democracy. Nature, extent and ends of participation depends not only on the organizational structure but also practicing the principles of democracy. Hence, it is suggested that the democratic principles should be effectively practiced in the deliberations of the participative forums of both the organizations. Non-implementation of all the decisions, delay in implementation of decisions were more in BHEL than in TISCO. This shows absence of top management's commitment and support to the schemes in BHEL. It is viewed that the effective functioning of participative management is next to impossibility without top managements's commitment and support. It is, therefore, suggested that the top management of BHEL should be committed to and render its support in order to enjoy the fruits of the participative management. This suggestion is also applicable to TISCO for furtherance of effectiveness of functioning of the scheme.

Impact of Participative Management

Workers' participation is based on the democratic principles of equity, equality and justice. Participation provides an opportunity to the workers at the helm of affairs to share their experiences and knowledge with managers. It is being increasingly resorted to all over the world to supplement contact relationship, as it provides quality of work life and satisfies the legitimate expectations of workers[1]. The basic premise of participation is that a worker who invests his human resources in his company has at least as much right to say in tis management as a shareholder who invests capital.[2] According to Douglas Mc Gregor, workers' participation in management is "a formal method of providing an opportunity for every member of the organization to contribute his brain and ingenuity as well as has physical efforts fro the improvement of organizational effectiveness, as well as enhancing his own economic welfare.[3]

In the words of V.V. Giri, "such an association of labour and management at all levels would lead to promotion of increased productivity for the general benefit of the enterprise, the employers and community, giving employee better understanding of their role in the

1. Patil, S. M., "Participative Management - Mechnaics of Workers' participation," *Indian Journal of Industrial Relations*, Vol. 7, No.1, July, 1971, p. 112.
2. Ramesh, K. and Narasimha Rao, GBVL., *op.cit.*, pp. 5-6.
3. Mc Gregor, Douglas, "The Human Side of Enterprise", McGraw Hill Book Co., New York, 1960, p. 113.

working of the industry, and in the process of production, satisfaction of the urge for self-expression in employees, thus, leading to industrial peace. Better relations and increased co-operation, will enable employers to win their confidence and co-operation. Such association of labour with management in a real way at all levels will break the barriers between labour and management and do away with suspicion and mistrust and replace antagonism with co-operation."[1] Workers' participation in management has its impact mainly on organizational and individual goals. However, it influences the social goals also indirectly. It contributes to the achievement of individual goals effectively by providing a conducive climate for satisfying workers' urge for self-expression and overall personality development. It also enhances the skills of understanding and maintaining human relations through free and open communication and discussion. In turn it helps for the development of human resources of an organization. It is needless to say that workers' participation in management leads to the improvement of the economic well-being of workers. Thus workers' participation in management has its impact on satisfying the workers economic, social and psychological needs.

The satisfied and developed human resources through the process of workers' participation in management are expected to enhance their contributions to the effective achievement of organizational goals. These goals include sound industrial relations, providing better working conditions, taking care of welfare of the employees, elimination of sense of alienation of the workers, maximizing productivity[2] and profitability.

Against this backdrop, it is proposed to study the impact of participative management on the organizations through its impact on (a) sense of alienation of the workers (b) Labour welfare and safety (c) Industrial relation and (d) Production and its efficiency.

But, it is highly difficult to measure the impact of participative management quantitatively on the various aspects of an organization. Hence, the opinions,[3] attitudes[4] and perceptions[5] of the worker and

1. Giri, V.V., op.cit., p. 10.
2. Davis, Keith, "Human Behaviour At Work," Tata McGraw-Hill Publishing Co., Limited, New Delhi, p. 160.
3. A belief component is usually called an opinion (Morgan, Clifford, T., King Richard A., and Robinson, Nancy, M., "Industrial Psychology," Tata McGraw Hill Publishing Co. Ltd., New Delhi, 1882, p. 451.
4. A learned Predisposition to be have in a consistent evaluative manner toward a person, a group of People, an object. (Ibid).
5. Perception refers to a Person's immediate experience of an object (Ibid).

management representatives (who are also the members of the participative management) are taken up as basis to analyze the impact of participative management on the four aspects mentioned earlier of BHEL and TISCO.

The dimensions of elimination of the sense of alienation include improvement in the workers sense of responsibility and maturity, a change in the workers attitude to oppose/resist changes in production and organizational structure, reduction in the workers sense of powerlessness and increase in the sense of involvement.

The factors which influence the working conditions and labour welfare are, improvement in working conditions, improvement in safety, and improvement in health, housing, welfare facilities etc.

Sound industrial relations include improvement in general discipline, resolution of disputes and grievances, improvement in communication between workers and management and improvement in relation between labour and management with better rapport.

Increase in production and its efficiency includes factors such as increase in output, reduction in cost of raw material per unit of output, elimination of wastage, optimum utilization of man-machine capacity, improvement in the quality of production, reduction in absenteeism etc. Increase in productivity normally enhances profitability of the organization and earnings of the workers.

Impact of Participative Management on Elimination of the Sense of Alienation

Alienation may result from poor design of socio-technical systems.[1] The work system is being planned by some one end the employee has to follow it without understanding the whys and whats of his role towards the finished product. Consequently the employee doesn't have adequate command over the entire operation. Employees feel that they are not fit for anything. When these feelings become substantial, an employee may develop adverse psychological feelings. This psychological state is called alienation.[2] Alienation contains ingredients like feelings of powerlessness, lack of meaning, loneliness, disorientation and lack of attachment to job, work group, or organisation.[3]

1. Davis, Keith, *op.cit*. p. 273.
2. *Ibid.*
3. *Ibid.*

Alienated people often tend to withdraw from reality and live in a detached world. Participative management plays a critical role in the elimination of the sense of alienation. It delegates the power to share information, and the authority to discuss, create facilities to discuss in social environment and to understand the entire process of production. Moreover, it encourages the employee to interact with and understand each other. Consequently, it reduces the sense of alienation. Here an attempt has been made to find out the impact of participative management on the reduction of sense of alienation. Five areas of alienation *viz.*, (i) increase in workers' sense of responsibility (ii) reduction of workers attitude of resistance to change (iii) reduction in workers' sense of powerlessness (iv) increase in workers' sense of involvement in work/ factory (v) increase in workers' sense of satisfaction are taken up to find out the impact of participative management on elimination of sense of alienation. Table 4.1 depicts the perception/opinions of the members regarding the impact of participative management on elimination of sense of alienation.

The feeling of oneness and the close association of workers with the management help develop a sense of responsibility for the job as well as for the organization. Participative management has significantly contributed to the raise of workers' sense of responsibility towards the work as perceived by 63.34 per cent of management representatives and 46.67 per cent of workers' representatives from BHEL and 53.06 per cent of management representatives and 43.88 per cent of workers' members from TISCO. The remaining representatives felt that the workers' participation in management in the units did not have any impact. It may be due to absence of delegation of required authority and responsibility to the participants of workers' participation in management. Hence, it is suggested that the management should delegate required authority and make the workers feel a sense of responsibility.

Organizations normally introduce changes to meet the changing needs of the customers. Employees resist the change because the changes require them to acquire new skills and knowledge and to adapt themselves to the new environment. Participative management helps to reduce resistance to change. According to Davis, "A fundamental way to build support for change is through participation. It encourages employees to discuss, to communicate, to make suggestion, and to become interested in change. Participation encourages commitment rather than mere compliance with change. Commitment implies motivation to support a

Table 4.1 : Impact of Participative Management of Elimination of Sense of Alienation

(*Members responses are indicated in percentage*)

Areas of Elimination of Sense Alienation	Nature of Impact Perceived by Respondents															
	BHEL (N=30)								TISCO (N=98)							
	Positive		*No Impact*		*Uncertain*		*Total*		*Positive*		*Impact*		*Uncertain*		*Total*	
	MR	WR	MR	WR	MR	WR	MR	WR	MR	WR	MR	WR	MR	WR	MR	WR
Increase in workers sense of responsibility	63.34	46.67	33.33	43.33	3.33	10.00	100.00	100.00	53.06	43.88	39.80	47.96	7.14	8.16	100.00	100.00
Reduction in Workers Attitude of resistance to change	66.67	46.67	23.33	43.33	10.99	10.00	100.00	100.00	58.16	45.92	36.73	40.82	5.11	13.26	100.00	100.00
Reduction in workers sense of powerless	60.00	46.67	26.67	36.66	13.33	16.67	100.00	100.00	64.29	48.98	31.63	39.00	4.08	11.22	100.00	100.00
Increase in Workers sense of involvement in work/factory	73.33	50.00	20.00	40.00	6.67	10.00	100.00	100.00	70.41	54.08	19.39	35.72	10.20	10.20	100.00	100.00
Increase in workers sense of satisfaction	76.67	46.67	16.67	36.67	6.66	16.66	100.00	100.00	60.20	57.14	22.45	36.74	17.35	6.12	100.00	100.00
Average(Elimination of sense of alienation)	68.00	46.67	24.00	40.67	8.00	12.66	100.00	100.00	61.22	50.00	30.00	40.21	8.78	9.79	100.00	100.00

M.R. : Management Representatives; W.R. : Workers' Representatives. **Source** : Data is collected through questionnaire.

Note : Negative Impact is not perceived by respondents.

change and work to assure that it operates effectively."[1] An attempt has been made to enquire about the impact of participative management on the reduction of resistance to change.

It is observed from this table that 66.67 per cent of management representatives, 46.67 per cent of workers' representatives from BHEL and 58.16 per cent of management representatives. 45.92 per cent of workers' representatives from TISCO, perceived that participative management helped to reduce the resistance to change. However, a considerable number of respondents did not visualize any impact of participative management in this regard. This may be due to the non-supply of complete information to workers representatives and not considering their opinions on plans and programmes of change. Hence, it is suggested that the management should supply all relevant information to workers and give due consideration to the points of view of their representatives about implementation of change.

The feeling of an individual that he has no capacity to effect management policies and rules, job conditions and immediate work processes,[2] is referred to as powerlessness. Participative management helps the members to participate in the management process, programmes, decision-making etc. Thus, participative management provides some power to their employees, which reduces the feeling of powerlessness.

It is observed from the table that 60.00 per cent of the management representatives, 46.67 per cent of the workers' representatives, from BHEL and 64.29 per cent of the management representatives and 48.98 per cent of the workers representatives from TISCO felt that the participative management reduced the feeling of powerlessness. That participative management did not contribute at all to the reduction of sense of powerlessness among employees was expressed by 31.67 per cent of the members from BHEL and 35.71 per cent members from TISCO. The remaining respondents did not see any clear impact, which may be due to the lack of authority or carelessness of management in recognizing the power of workers' representatives. This type of practice on the part of management hampers the very purpose of workers' participation in management. Hence, it is suggested that the management should make the workers feel their importance in the organization.

1. *Ibid.*, p. 213.
2. Dale S. Beach, *op.cit.*, p. 36.

The sense of involvement of the workmen in the job significantly depends on participative management. The effectiveness of participative management in increasing the sense of involvement in work is positive as expressed by 73.33 per cent of management representatives, 50.00 per cent of workers representatives from BHEL and 70.41 per cent from Management and 54.08 per cent of workers representatives from TISCO. Thus about half of the workers' representatives feel that the workers' participation in management did not improve their sense of involvement in work. This might be due to the absence of sense of belonging. The sense of belonging can be improved by involving the workers psychologically and socially in workers' participation in management.

Mean scores explain that the majority of the management representatives 64.61 per cent from both the organizations perceived that there is a positive impact of participative management on elimination of sense of alienation. Thus it can be viewed that the impact of participative management in the elimination of sense of alienation is positive and significant as viewed by management representatives. It is more in BHEL than in TISCO. It is observed that workers' participation in management did not eliminate their sense of alienation. This feeling is more in BHEL than in TISCO. The majority of the management representatives in public sector and more number of the workers representatives in private sector perceived positive impact. Hence it is suggested that the management should involve the representatives of workers' participation in management not only physically but also psychologically and socially.

Impact of Participative Management on Working Conditions and Welfare Facilities

Labour welfare means anything done for the comfort and improvement—intellectual or social—of the employees, over and above the wages paid.[1] The logic behind providing welfare facilities is to create an efficient, healthy, loyal and satisfied labour force for the organization and also for the nation. Welfare services are not a charity, but are essential to get higher productivity from the workers by satisfying their needs.

Working conditions and welfare facilities include proper lighting, heat control, cleanliness, low noise level, toilet and drinking water facilities, canteen and rest rooms, health and safety measures, reasonable hours of work and holidays and welfare services, such as housing,

1. Arthur James Todd, "A Sociological Appraisal of Modern Industrialization."

education, recreation, transportation and counselling.[1]

Providing certain facilities is a legal obligation and providing some more facilities is a social obligation of the organization. Management knows the workers' reactions to the existing facilities and their demand for new facilities through interactions in participative management meetings. In fact, one of the objectives of participative management is to improve the working and welfare facilities. Thus the welfare and working conditions are influenced by several factors like Government's statutory obligations, social obligations, demand of the employees for such facilities in collective bargaining and workers' participation in management meetings etc. An attempt has been made to find out the impact of participative management on welfare and working conditions. Table 3.26 shows the number of items discussed in participative management meetings on working conditions and welfare facilities. It is observed from the table that out of 4,200 items discussed in BHEL, 1,840 (43.81 per cent) items relate to welfare and safety. Whereas 29.40 per cent (11,326 out of 38,524) of items relate to welfare and safety in TISCO. Thus a significant number of items relating to welfare is discussed in workers' participation in management meetings which shows the impact of participative management on working conditions in those two organizations. It is more in BHEL than in TISCO. However, the impact of workers' participation in management on welfare facilities can be analyzed clearly based on the respondent's opinions in this regard.

Table 4.2 depicts the respondent's perception/attitude towards the impact of participative management on the improvement of working conditions and welfare facilities. Three areas which show this impact are (i) improvement in working conditions, (ii) improvement in safety and (iii) improvement in health, housing and welfare facilities.

It is observed from the table that 53.33 per cent of the management representatives and 40.00 per cent of the worker representatives from BHEL and 62.25 per cent of the management representatives and 23.47 per cent of the workers' representatives from TISCO felt the impact of participative management on working conditions positively.

The participative management has contributed positively to the safety as opined by 63.33 per cent of management representatives, 53.34 per cent of workers' representatives from BHEL and 68.37 per cent of management representatives, 59.18 per cent of workers' representatives from TISCO.

1. Monappa, Arun & Sayaddin Mirza, S., "*Personnel Management*" Tata McGraw-Hill Publishing Co. Ltd., New Delhi, 1990, p. 217.

Table 4.2 : Impact of Participative Management on Improvement of Working Conditions and Welfare

(Members responses are indicated in percentage)

Areas of Improvement of working conditions and welfare	Nature of Impact Perceived by Respondents															
	BHEL (N=30)								TISCO (N=98)							
	Positive		*No Impact*		*Uncertain*		*Total*		*Positive*		*Impact*		*Uncertain*		*Total*	
	MR	WR	MR	WR	MR	WR	MR	WR	MR	WR	MR	WR	MR	WR	MR	WR
Improvement in working conditions	53.33	40.00	23.33	43.33	23.34	16.67	100.00	100.00	62.25	23.47	8.16	20.41	19.59	56.12	100.00	100.00
Improvement in Safety	63.33	53.34	16.67	23.33	20.00	23.33	100.00	100.00	68.37	59.18	10.20	12.25	21.43	28.57	100.00	100.00
Improvement in Health, housing and welfare	73.33	63.34	10.00	23.33	16.67	13.33	100.00	100.00	70.41	63.26	7.14	12.25	22.45	24.49	100.00	100.00
Average (working conditions and welfare)	63.33	52.22	16.67	30.00	20.00	17.78	100.00	100.00	67.01	48.64	8.50	14.97	24.49	36.39	100.00	100.00

M.R. : Management Representatives; W.R. : Workers' Representatives. **Source** : Data is collected through questionnaire.

Note : Negative Impact is not perceived by respondents.

Provision of health, housing and welfare to the employees is of vital importance in any organization. The majority of the respondents i.e., 73.33 per cent of management representatives, 63.34 per cent of workers representatives from BHEL and 70.41 per cent of management representatives, 63.26 per cent of workers' representatives from TISCO perceived that participative management has contributed significantly to health, housing and welfare facilities.

The remaining respondents did not have a clear idea about the impact of participative management on working conditions and welfare facilities.

The mean scores explain that the participative management has contributed positively to working conditions and welfare as perceived by 63.33 per cent of management representatives, 52.22 per cent of workers' representatives from BHEL and 67.00 per cent of management representatives, 48.64 percent of workers' representatives from TISCO.

Thus, it can be viewed that the participative management has contributed significantly to the improvement of working conditions and welfare facilities, as perceived by management representatives. It is also observed that baout half of the workers' representatives felt that workers' participation in management did not improve the working conditions and welfare facilities. This feeling is more in TISCO than in BHEL. The majority of the management representatives from TISCO and the majority of workers' representatives from BHEL reported a positive impact. It is suggested that, the management should be considerate in improving the welfare facilities through the means of workers' participation in management.

Impact of Participative Management on Industrial Relations

"Industrial relation is the composite result of the attitude and approaches of employers and employees towards each other with regard to planning, supervision, direction and co-ordination of the activities of an organization with a minimum of human effects and frictions with an organization with a minimum of human effects and frictions with an animating spirit of co-operation and with proper regard for the genuine well-being of all members of the organization."[1] The creation and maintenance of good relations between the workers and the management is the very basis on which the industrial democracy depends. Industrial

1. Ordway, Teade & Metcalfe, "*Personnel Administration—Its Principles and Practice*," 1970, p. 2.

democracy to a greater extend can be achieved through workers' participation in management. The purpose of participative management, as stated in the second Five Year Plan[1], are satisfying the workers' urge for self expression, thus, leading to industrial peace, better participative relations and increased co-operation. The need for maintaining cordial industrial relations is to attain industrial peace, for fair treatment to workers and to achieve higher production etc.

Industrial relations are influenced by several factors like attitude, and organization of trade unions, socio-economic atmosphere in the country, and the relation between price, wages and profits etc. Four sub-areas i.e. (i) improvement in general discipline, (ii) resolution of grievances and disputes, (iii) improvement in communication between management and workers and (iv) improvement in relations between workers and management are identified as criteria to find out the impact of workers' participation in management on industrial relations.

The members' opinions/perceptions regarding the impact of participative management on sound industrial relations are presented in Table 4.3.

The majority of the members from both the organizations i.e., 73.34 per cent of management representatives, 63.33 per cent of workers representatives from BHEL and 97.96 per cent of management representatives, 94.90 per cent of workers' representatives from TISCO, perceived that the participative management has contributed significantly to the improvement of general discipline.

Speedy redressal of grievances and disputes improve the industrial relation situation. The impact of participative management on the redressal of grievances and disputes is positive as expressed by 86.66 per cent of management representatives, 73.33 per cent of workers' representatives from BHEL and 94.90 per cent of management representatives, 95.92 per cent of workers' representatives from TISCO. Here it is interesting to observe that more worker representatives in TISCO have expressed that there is a positive impact of participative management on resolution of grievances and disputes in time than those of management representatives.

Communication means getting across ideas and information to another person. Communication is important in an organization because it helps to exchange ideas and to work together.[2]

1. Govt. of India, Second Five Year Plan. *op.cit.*, p. 577.
2. Monappa Arun, Saiyadain Mirza, S., op.cit., p. 255.

Table 4.3 : Impact of Participative Management on Industrial Relations

(*Members responses are indicated in percentage*)

Areas of Industrial Relations	Nature of Impact Perceived by Respondents															
	BHEL (N=30)								TISCO (N=98)							
	Positive		*No Impact*		*Uncertain*		*Total*		*Positive*		*Impact*		*Uncertain*		*Total*	
	MR	WR	MR	WR	MR	WR	MR	WR	MR	WR	MR	WR	MR	WR	MR	WR
Improvement in general discipline	73.34	63.33	13.33	26.67	13.33	10.00	100.00	100.00	97.96	94.90	--	2.04	2.04	3.06	100.00	100.00
Resolution of grievances and disputes	86.66	73.33	6.67	16.67	6.67	10.00	100.00	100.00	94.90	95.92	2.04	2.04	3.06	2.04	100.00	100.00
Improvement in communication between workers and management	93.33	66.67	--	20.00	6.67	13.33	100.00	100.00	100.00	93.88	--	4.08	--	2.04	100.00	100.00
Improvement in relations between workers and management	80.00	70.00	6.67	13.33	13.33	16.67	100.00	100.00	95.92	92.86	--	5.10	4.08	2.04	100.00	100.00
Average (Industrial Relations	83.33	68.33	6.67	19.17	10.00	12.50	100.00	100.00	97.19	94.39	0.51	3.32	2.30	2.29	100.00	100.00

M.R. : Management Representatives; W.R. : Workers' Representatives. **Source** : Data is collected through questionnaire.

Note : Negative Impact is not perceived by respondents.

Workers' participation in management contributes to improvement in communication as majority of the respondents i.e., 93.33 per cent of management representatives, 66.67 cent of workers' representatives from BHEL and cent per cent of management representatives, 93.99 per cent of workers' representatives from TISCO perceived that workers' participation in management has contributed for the effective communication. It is suggested that the management of BHEL should take all possible care to improve communication significantly.

Maintenance of cordial relations between employer and employee is highly essential for the smooth running of an organization. Majority of the member i.e., 80 per cent of management representatives, 70 per cent of workers' representatives from BHEL and 95.92 per cent of management representatives, 92.86 per cent of workers' representatives from TISCO reported that the participative management has contributed significantly to the maintenance of congenial industrial relations. However, more than 20 per cent of the representatives from BHEL viewed that the participative management did not have positive impact on industrial relations.

It is observed form the mean scores that the number of management representatives who perceived that the impact of participative management on industrial relations is positive is more than the workers' representatives.

It may be concluded that the impact of participative management is high on the industrial relations in both the organizations. But the effectiveness is more in TISCO than in BHEL as perceived by the respondents. Hence, it is suggested that management of BHEL should also concentrate on improving employer-employee relations through workers' participation in management.

Impact of Participative Management on Production and Productivity

The purpose of workers' participation in management, in the words of the Second Five-Year-Plan is to increase productivity for the general benefit of the enterprise, the employees and the community.[1] Thus, the main objectives of the scheme of workers' participation in management in India are to achieve higher production and productivity.

The production and productivity is influenced by a number of factors besides participative management, viz., changes in technology,

1. Govt. of India, Second Five Year Plan, *op.cit.*, p. 577.

management skill and ability, flow and availability of suitable human and capital resources, proper political and social climate and industrial policy of the Government, size of the market, enthusiasm and sense of belonging of workers. In fact, productivity has two aspects[1] *viz.*, technical and human. The technical aspect relates to technique of better organization and better management, whereas the human aspect relates to social and psychological aspects of the workers. Psychological and social aspects require better attitude, motivation, industrial relations, monetary and social incentives and security of tenure, living wage, scope for promotion etc. Workers' participation in management provides the environment to the workers to realize their social and psychological needs there by maximizing their contribution to increase in productivity. As discussed in Chapter 3, the functioning of the scheme of workers' participation in management in the two organizations under study might have influenced various aspects of production and productivity through human aspects.

Seven aspects of production and productivity i.e. *i)* out-put *ii)* cost of production, *iii)* wastage *iv)* utilization of raw material *v)* utilization of man-machine capacity *vi)* quality of output and *vii)* absenteeism are identified as measures to find out the impact of participative management on production and productivity.

The output of both the organizations is shown in Table 4.4. It can be observed from the table that the output (physical units) has significantly increased from by 233.41 per cent in BHEL whereas it went up by 31.30 per cent in TISCO during the period 1980-81 to 1988-89. The output in monetary units increased from Rs. 1302.60 millions to Rs. 4403.00 millions (or by 238.02 per cent) in BHEL whilst it rose up from Rs. 5208.60 million to Rs. 18617.70 millions (or by 257.44 per cent) in TISCO during the period understudy. The labour productivity (Table 4.5) has also significantly increased from Rs. 0.13 millions in 1981-82 to Rs. 0.42 millions in 1988-89 in BHEL and from Rs. 0.10 millions to Rs. 0.24 millions in TISCO during the same period. However, it is difficult to conclude that the increase in productivity during the period is due to the impact of workers' participation in management. Hence, an attempt is made to find out the opinions of the respondents in this regard.

The opinions of the members on the impact of participative management on the increase in production and productivity are presented in Table 4.6.

1. Gopal, Vishnu, *op.cit.*, p. 387.

Table 4.4 : Growth of Output in BHEL and TISCO during 1980–81 to 1988–89

(Index Numbers only)

Year	BHEL	TISCO
1980-81	100.00	100.00
1981-82	110.35	106.12
1982-83	138.72	107.19
1983-84	181.14	105.87
1984-85	234.47	110.45
1985-86	279.62	110.64
1986-87	N.A	120.78
1987-88	294.78	123.45
1988-89	333.41	131.30

Note : Index Numbers are calculated with base year 1980-81=100

Source : Annual Reports of BHEL and TISCO

N.A. : Not Available.

Table 4.5 : Labour Productivity of BHEL and TISCO

(in millions of Rupees)

Year	BHEL	TISCO
1981-82	0.13	0.10
1982-83	0.18	0.11
1983-84	0.30	0.12
1984-85	0.29	0.15
1985-86	0.35	0.17
1986-87	N.A	0.20
1987-88	0.37	0.21
1988-89	0.42	0.24

Note : Labour productivity is calculated by dividing the production value (in millions of Rupees) by the average number of employees.

Source : Annual Reports of BHEL and TISCO for the above years

N.A. : Not Available.

Table 4.6 : Impact of Participative Management on Production and Productivity

(Members' responses are indicated in percentage)

Areas of Production and Productivity	Nature of Impact Perceived by Respondents															
	BHEL (N=30)								TISCO (N=98)							
	Positive		*No Impact*		*Uncertain*		*Total*		*Positive*		*Impact*		*Uncertain*		*Total*	
	MR	WR	MR	WR	MR	WR	MR	WR	MR	WR	MR	WR	MR	WR	MR	WR
Increase in output	90.00	63.33	10.00	20.00	--	16.67	100.00	100.00	76.53	59.18	20.40	31.63	3.07	9.19	100.00	100.00
Reduction in cost of production	60.00	46.67	30.00	40.00	10.00	13.33	100.00	100.00	68.37	47.96	21.43	32.65	10.20	19.39	100.00	100.00
Elimination of wastage	63.33	53.33	23.34	30.00	13.33	16.67	100.00	100.00	65.30	54.08	17.35	23.47	17.35	22.45	100.00	100.00
Optimum utilization of Raw Materials	70.00	60.00	10.00	26.67	20.00	13.33	100.00	100.00	82.65	68.37	8.16	21.43	9.19	10.20	100.00	100.00
Optimum utilization of Man Machine Capacity	73.34	56.67	13.33	23.33	13.33	20.00	100.00	100.00	73.47	69.39	10.20	18.37	16.33	12.24	100.00	100.00
Improvement in quality of output	63.33	50.00	20.00	33.33	16.67	16.67	100.00	100.00	75.51	67.35	9.18	14.29	15.31	18.37	100.00	100.00
Reduction in absenteeism	76.67	66.67	13.33	16.67	10.00	16.67	100.00	100.00	86.73	83.67	3.06	7.15	10.21	9.18	100.00	100.00
Average(Production and Productivity	70.95	56.67	17.15	27.14	11.90	16.19	100.00	100.00	75.51	64.29	12.83	21.28	11.66	14.43	100.00	100.00

M.R. : Management Representatives; W.R. : Workers' Representatives **Source** : Data is collected through questionnaire.

Note : Negative Impact is not perceived by respondents.

The majority of the members form both the organizations i.e. 90.00 per cent of management representatives, 63.33 per cent of workers' representatives from BHEL and 76.53 per cent of management representatives and 59.18 per cent of workers' representatives from TISCO perceived that the impact of participative management on output is significant. As many as 15.00 per cent of members from BHEL and 26.02 per cent members from TISCO stated that there is no impact of participative management on production and productivity. Only 16.67 per cent of workers' representatives from BHEL and 3.07 per cent of management representatives, 9.19 per cent of workers' representatives from TISCO opined that they are uncertain about the impact of participative management on production and productivity.

The above analysis clearly shows that the functioning of workers' participation in management is a significant factor responsible for the increase in production and productivity in both the organizations. However, it is more so in BHEL.

Sharing of experiences and implementation of suggestions offered in the process of participation help in reduction of cost of production. It is observed from the table that 60 per cent of management representatives, 46.67 per cent of workers' representatives from BHEL and 68.37 per cent of management representatives, 47.96 per cent of workers' representatives from TISCO perceived the participative management has contributed to reduction in cost and improvement in production. The members who expressed that there is no impact of participative management on cost of production include 35.00 per cent of members from BHEL and 27.04 per cent of members from TISCO. Only 10.00 per cent of management representatives, 13.33 percent of workers' representatives from BHEL and 10.20 per cent of management representatives, 19.39 per cent of workers' representatives from TISCO have stated that they are uncertain about the impact of participative management on the cost of production. It is clear from the above analysis that the participative management has a remarkable influence on reduction of cost of production.

Wastage in the production process influences the productivity and cost of production of and organization. Hence, the elimination of wastage is also to be one of the objectives of workers' participation in management. It is clear form the table that 58.33 per cent members form BHEL and 59.69 per cent of members from TISCO viewed that the participative management has positive impact on the elimination of wastage. However nearly one-fourth of the respondents viewed that the influence of participative management on reduction of wastage is unclear.

Optimum utilization of raw materials is essential for any organization. The impact of participative management on utilization of raw material is considerable as opined by 70.00 per cent of management representatives, 60.00 per cent of workers' representatives from BHEL and 82.65 per cent of management representatives, 68.37 per cent of workers' representatives from TISCO. As many as 18.33 per cent of members from BHEL and 14.80 per cent members from TISCO have stated that there is no impact of participative management. Nearly one-tenth of the members were not sure of the impact of participative management in this regard.

Another sub-area for production and productivity is optimum utilization of man-machine capacity. On this the majority of the members i.e. 73.34 per cent of management representatives, 56.67 per cent of workers' representatives from BHEL and 73.47 per cent of management representatives, 69.39 per cent of workers' representatives from TISCO expressed that because of participative management, the optimum utilization of man-machine capacity was possible. Other members did not express positive impact in this regard.

Absenteeism means absence of workers from their regular work without prior permission, notice or sanction.[1] It is an important problem in any enterprise. Excessive absenteeism adversely affects work and delivery schedules and cost of manpower, in addition to productivity. The objective of the workers' participation in management is to improve production and productivity. The rate of absenteeism is to be reduced to attain this objective. In the participative forum meetings, the members often discuss the problem of absenteeism. The opinions of the members on the impact of workers' participation in management on absenteeism have been obtained. The majority of the members from both the organization i.e. 71.67 per cent of members from BHEL and 85.20 per cent of members from TISCO, perceived that the participative management has significantly reduced the absenteeism in their organizations.

Mean scores explain that the majority of the management representatives (70.95 per cent) from BHEL and (75.51 per cent) from TISCO perceived that the participative management has contributed significantly and these percentage were higher than that of the workers' representatives (56.67 per cent) from BHEL and (64.29 per cent) from TISCO.

1. B.P. Singh et at. *op.cit.*, p. 349.

To sum up, the impact of participative management on the production and productivity is significant. Management representatives are more satisfied with the concept and performance of participative management then workers' representatives. This may be due to lack of proper understanding among workers' representatives about the concept and impact of participative management on various aspects of the organization. Hence, it is suggested that the management should undertake educational and training programmes to enrich the human resources of the workers in the areas of participative management. These programmes will help the workers to develop a positive attitude about the impact of participative management and improve their contributions to the organizational goals viz., industrial relations and productivity.

Conclusion

Workers' participation in management—a technique of personnel management and industrial relations—is expected to contribute not only to the effective management of personnel and the maintenance of sound industrial relations but also to the achievement of individual and organizations at goals like productivity. The contribution of the workers' participation in management can be analyzed through its impact. It is evident from the above analysis that workers' participation in management has its impact on the maintenance of sound industrial relations, as also on the goals of individual employees and organization. But the workers representatives did not find much impact unlike management representatives. This is possibly due to lack of clear idea about the role of workers' participation in management and inability of the workers to view the entire process of the system, which may be a hindrance to the successful functioning of workers' participation in management. Hence, it is suggested that the management should provide extensive education to the workers about the entire process of workers' participation in management.

Further, it is clear that the impact is relatively more positive in TISCO than in BHEL. Though the BHEL - a Public Sector Unit, is expected to be a model employer, it could not be a model to the TISCO. In fact TISCO played a model role to the BHEL in workers' participation in management. This may be due to the structural convenience and adaptability in TISCO and commitment of top management of TISCO. These are the limitations to BHEL as it is a public sector unit. Hence, it is suggested that the Government should provide these convenience to public sector units for effective functioning of workers' participation in management in those units.

Quality Circles

Quality circle is a small group phenomenon. It is a group of employees belonging to the same work area, or doing similar type of work, meeting voluntarily and regularly to identify, analyze and resolve work-related problems. It is basically a problem-solving and decision-making group and an extension to workers' participation in management.

Origin and Growth of Quality Circles in BHEL and TISCO

Quality circle is basically a problem-solving and participative and decision-making group of a few employees working in a unit of an organization. The quality circle movement in India was started in BHEL, Hyderabad unit, in 1981. Mr. Udpa, the then General Manager (Operations), BHEL, Hyderabad, in one of his business visits to Japan, observed the functioning of Quality Circles (QCs) in than country as he was interested in the concept and philosophy. He held discussions with Prof. Shin Miura of Tamagawa University on the subject. After returning to India, Mr. Udpa discussed with different managers of BHEL his experiences and the feasibility of starting quality circles in BHEL.

In the initial, formation stage, there were doubts among the employees and mangers of the BHEL about the success of quality circles. Mr. Udpa presented the quality circle concept to the senior executives on 27th October 1980, and they showed enthusiasm towards this system. A steering committee was formed on 28th October 1980 and the workers and executives of two different work areas (i.e., one from the production department and one from the service department) were exposed to this concept. The workers came forward to form into five circles i.e., three manufacturing and two purchasing involving 42 members after several hours of discussions. The steering committee gave relevant training on varied aspects of quality circles including statistical Quality Control[1] techniques. Five quality circles were formally inaugurated on 5th January, 1981. The first presentation to the top management about the achievements of the circles was organized by the workers within three months of inauguration. The other major events that took place during this stage in the unit are: organization of a training programme for leaders, deputy leaders and facilitators (July, 1981); inauguration of the second batch of 12 quality circles (August, 1981); inauguration of the third batch of 16 quality circles and commencement of publication of "Q circle Forum"—a quarterly newsletter (January, 1982); a visit by the Union Minister for Industries, Steel and Mines to observe quality circle progress (July, 1982); inauguration of the fourth batch of 18 quality circles (August, 1982); inauguration of the fifth batch of 24 circles (October, 1982); and inauguration of the sixth batch of nine QCs (December, 1982). During this stage QCs made rapid progress; the number rose to 106, and they spread not only to different manufacturing shops but also to the various service departments such as personnel. Training, Hospital, Township, Administration and Quality Control.

In the second stage i.e., in the stabilization stage, the first Annual quality circles convention[2] was organized in August by the unit in order to: (i) recognize the efforts of QCs; (ii) encourage healthy competition between them in different units; (iii) exchange experience; and (iv) institutionalize the concept and make it a way of life. The Hyderabad unit received three awards for the best case studies and a trophy for the best promotion of QCs during the year 1982-83. The other events which took place during this stage are: organization of a meeting of an apex level joint committee, which recommended an annual growth rate of 15 per cent in QC membership (July, 1984): presentation of a paper by the General Manager on stabilization of QCs in an international conference (Septem-

1. The Statistical Quality Control techniques are simple problem-solving techniques used by quality circles to identify, analyse and resolve problems. The are Brain storming, Data Collection, Pareto analysis, Cause and Effect Diagram, Line Graphs, Frequency Distribution, Scatter Diagram and Histogram.
2. Dwivedi, R.S., "Effectiveness of Quality Circles and Its determinates in a Large Industrial Organisation in India," *Indian Journal of Industrial Relations*, Vol. 22, No. 4, April, 1987, p. 357.

ber, 1984); inauguration of the sixteenth batch of 42 QCs (March, 1985); and the seventeenth batch of 16 QCs (April, 1985). Thus growth in QC activities took place during the latter stabilization stage. Now there are 352 circles with a membership of 3513[1]. The two or three circles formed into a group to work together on a common problem and making a joint presentation was a characteristic feature of QC activity in BHEL.

The formation of Quality Circles in TISCO was thanks to their success in their sister concern i.e., TELCO, Jamshedpur, where QCs had been functioning effectively.[2] The model as well as its framework was based on the TELCO's model. The first batch of 12 quality circles was started in the year 1986. The quality circles introduced in TISCO are on an experimental basis.

Organization Structure of Quality Circles

The principal factor responsible for the success of any organization is its structural and functional support from among its different elements. A well structured approach is, there fore, absolutely necessary for success in case of quality circles also.

The organization structure of the quality circle sin BHEL is presented in Chart 5.1. As can be observed from the chart, the organization consists of non-members, members, circle leader and deputy leader, facilitators, steering committee, co-ordinator and top management. The functions and duties of the QC members are the same as discussed in Chapter-1.

The TISCO management has chalked out the structure of their quality circles according to their administrative convenience (Chart 5.2). The convenor is the head of the quality circle activities. He is assisted by Joint Convenor. The facilitators are directly involved in the Quality Circle activities, followed by leader, deputy leader, members and non-members. The duties and responsibilities of the members are similar to those discussed in Chapter-1.

Working of Quality Circles

1. Factors influencing the working

The effectiveness of the working of QCs depends on various factors like the length of experience of members in the QC, members awareness and environment in the meeting. Table 5.1 shows the respondents' length

1. BHEL, Quality Circle News, Quality Assurance Division, May, 1989.
2. Tata Steel, TISCO News, Public Relations Dept., Jamshedpur.

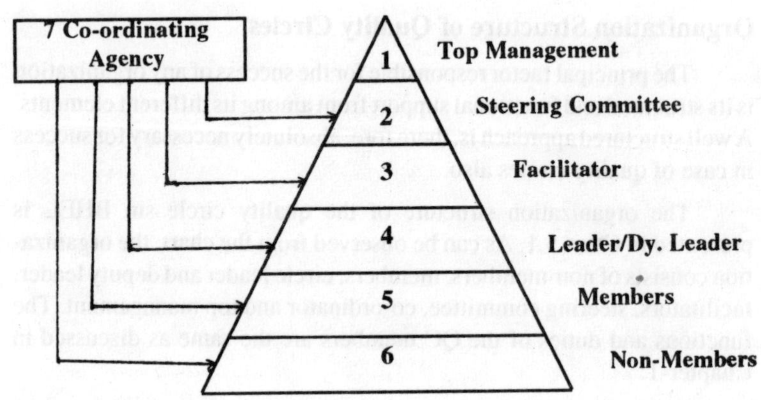

Chart 5.1

Structure of Quality Circles in BHEL

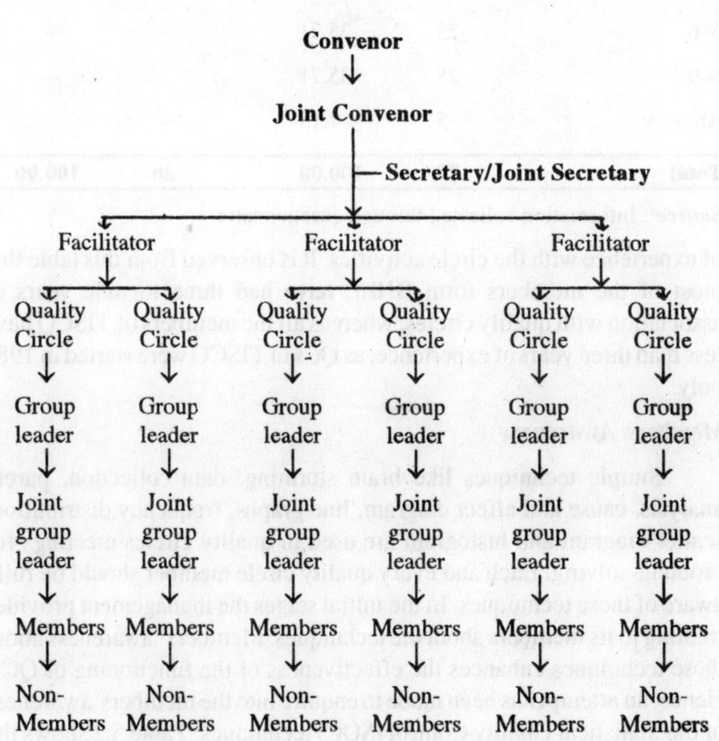

Source : Quality Assurance Division, TISCO.

Chart 5.2

Organization Structure of Quality Circles in TISCO

Table 5.1 : Span of Association of the Respondents with Quality Circles

Period	BHEL		TISCO	
(in Years)	Number	Per cent	Number	Per cent
Less than 3	15	21.43	20	100.00
3–6	25	35.71	--	--
6–9	25	35.71	--	--
Above 9	5	7.15	--	--
Total	**70**	**100.00**	**20**	**100.00**

Source : Information collected through questionnaire.

of experience with the circle activities. It is observed from this table that most of the members form BHEL have had three to nine years of association with quality circles, whereas all the members of TISCO have less than three years of experience, as QCs in TISCO were started in 1986 only.

Members' Awareness

Simple techniques like brain storming, data collection, pareto analysis, cause and effect diagram, line graphs, frequency distribution, scatter diagram and histogram are used in quality circles meetings for problem-solving. Each and every quality circle member should be fully aware of these techniques. In the initial stages the management provides training to its members about the techniques. Members' awareness about these techniques enhances the effectiveness of the functioning of QCs. Hence, an attempt has been made to enquire into the members' awareness of the Statistical Quality Control (SQC) techniques. Table 5.2 shows the awareness of the SQC Techniques to the respondents. It is observed from the table that majority of the members from both the organizations i.e., 94.29 per cent from BHEL and 90.00 per cent from TISCO stated that they are fully aware of the SQC techniques. Thus it is clear that the majority of the members are aware of the SQC techniques. The members' awareness of SQC techniques is better in BHEL than in TISCO, as opined by the members. However, it is suggested that the management should give proper training on the SQC techniques to the members who are unaware of it.

Environment in the Meeting

A congenial environment in the meetings plays a key role in the

Table 5.2 : Awareness of the Respondents about the 'SQC' Techniques

Awareness	BHEL		TISCO	
	Number	Per cent	Number	Per cent
Aware	66	94.29	18	90.00
Unaware	4	5.71	2	10.00
Total	**70**	**100.00**	**20**	**100.00**

Source : Information collected through questionnaire.

successful conduct of meetings. Further, a congenial climate in the meetings is necessary to improve the quality of the decisions. An enquiry has been made regarding the respondents' opinion about the environment in the meeting which is shown in the Table 5.3. The majority of the members i.e., 75.71 per cent from BHEL and 90.00 per cent from TISCO, expressed that the environment in the meetings is highly congenial. But as many as 17.15 per cent of the members from BHEL and 10.00 per cent of the members from TISCO expressed that the environment in the meetings remains congenial only for some time. However, a highly congenial environment is borne out by the majority opinion. The environment is more congenial in TISCO than in BHEL.

Table 5.3 : Respondents' Opinion on Evironment in the Meeting Place

Opinion	BHEL		TISCO	
	Number	Per cent	Number	Per cent
Always Congenial	53	75.71	18	90.00
Sometimes Congenial	12	17.15	2	10.00
Uncongenial	5	7.14	--	--
Total	**70**	**100.00**	**20**	**100.00**

Source : Information collected through questionnaire.

Quality circle prepares a list of problems that the members wish to tackle during the first meeting. The severity of the problem is determined by means of collecting data after the list is finalized. Various members take up assignments to collect the necessary data about the selected problem. Members fix the priority for analysis or for analyzing the problems after data collection is over. This process helps to take precautions so that a circle may not waste its time on minor problems or on the issues where solutions are already in process. Thus the first step in the working of the quality circle is listing and selection of problems for discussions.

Preparation of List of Items to be Discussed

The main objective of a quality circle is to identify, analyze and solve problems concerning quality, productivity, cost reduction, in the performance of the worker and enrichment of their work life.[1] Problems to be discussed are listed on the basis of the problems presented by the members and non-members.

A conducive environment generally enables the members to present the problems frequently in the meetings. An attempt was made to find out the frequency of problems presented. The responses of the employees are presented in Table 5.4. Majority of the members i.e., 64.29 per cent from BHEL and 75.00 per cent from TISCO, expressed that they proposed the issues frequently. A moderate proposal of the issues is done by 28.57 per cent members in BHEL and 20.00 per cent in TISCO. Only 7.14 per cent

Table 5.4 : Members' Proposals of the Issues

Frequency of the Proposal	BHEL		TISCO	
	Number	Per cent	Number	Per cent
Frequently	45	64.29	15	75.00
Moderately	20	28.57	4	20.00
Not at all	5	7.14	1	5.00
Total	**70**	**100.00**	**20**	**100.00**

Source : Information collected through questionnaire.

of the members from BHEL 5.00 per cent from TISCO expressed that they did not propose any issues at all. It is apparent that the conducive environment obtaining at their meetings enabled the members to present the problems frequently. A conducive environment also encourages the non-members to present the problems to leaders or members of the quality circles. In fact, non-members are also part of the quality circle organization. Table 5.5 shows the representations from non-members about the issues to be proposed. The majority of the members from both the organizations i.e., 44 (or 62.86 per cent) from BHEL and 13 (or 65 per cent) from TISCO, stated that they receive representations frequently from non-members. As many as 16 members (22.86 per cent) from BHEL

1. QCFI, Training for Quality Circles, p. 7.

Table 5.5 : Representations from Non-members (About the Issues to be Proposed)

Frequency of the representations	BHEL		TISCO	
	Number	Per cent	Number	Per cent
Frequent Representations	44	62.86	13	65.00
Representations now and then	16	22.86	5	25.00
No representations at all	10	14.28	20	10.00
Total	**70**	**100.00**	**20**	**100.00**

Source : Information collected through questionnaire.

and five members (25 per cent) from TISCO expressed that they received representations now and then from non-members on certain production related matters. Only a few members i.e., 14.28 per cent from BHEL and 10 per cent from TISCO, opined that they did not receive any representations from non-members. It is evident from the above table that representations by non-members are more frequent in TISCO than in BHEL. It is clear, therefore, that the non-members are also interested in the quality circle activities. However, it is suggested that the managements of both the organizations should further invite ideas from non-members.

Duration of the Meetings

The quality circle meetings are conducted during the working hours. Some times the members have to spend their off-the job-time on circle matters, i.e., during lunch hour. Here an attempt has been made to find out the members opinion on spending their own time on quality circle meetings. It is observed from the Table 5.6 that majority of the members from both the organizations i.e., 78.57 per cent from BHEL and 65 per cent from TISCO expressed that they did not spend their own time on the quality circle activities.

The quality circle members in both the organizations meet once a week for an hour[1]. Some times the duration of one hour may not be sufficient due to various reasons. Opinions of the members about the adequacy of the one hour duration to transact business are presented in the Table 5.7. It is clear from this Table that the majority of the members i.e., 64.29 per cent from BHEL and 80.00 per cent from TISCO, feel that

1. BHEL, Quality Circle, Quality Assurance Division and Tata Steel, Quality Assurance Division.

Table 5.6 : Sparing of Members' Own Time on Circle Meetings

Reasons	BHEL Number	BHEL Per cent	TISCO Number	TISCO Per cent
Spending	15	21.43	7	35.00
Not spending	55	78.57	13	65.00
Total	**70**	**100.00**	**20**	**100.00**

Source : Information collected through questionnaire.

Table 5.7 : Opinion on Adequacy of Present Time for the Meetings

Opinion	BHEL Number	BHEL Per cent	TISCO Number	TISCO Per cent
Adequate	45	64.29	16	80.00
Inadequate	25	35.71	4	20.00
Total	**70**	**100.00**	**20**	**100.00**

Source : Information collected through questionnaire.

the present duration of one hour as the meeting time is adequate. Only 35.71 per cent members from BHEL and 20 per cent from TISCO stated that the duration is inadequate.

It may be concluded that the majority of the members are satisfied with the present meeting time. The percentage of members who felt that the present time is inadequate is higher in BHEL than in TISCO.

The members who expressed their dissatisfaction with the duration of the meeting were asked about the desired length of time. Table 5.8 presents the members desired meeting time. The majority of the members i.e., 52.00 per cent form BHEL and 50.00 per cent from TISCO, felt that the time limit should be extended upto three hours. As many as 32.00 per cent members form BHEL and 25.00 per cent from TISCO expressed that the time limit for meetings should be extended to four hours. Only 16.00 per cent members from BHEL and 25.00 per cent members from TISCO opined that there should not be any time limit for meetings.

Thus, the majority of the members are of the opinion that the time limit for meetings should be three hours. It is further observed from the table that the members of both the organization expressed similar nature

Table 5.8 : Opinion of the Respondents on the Desired Time for the Meetings

	BHEL		TISCO	
Opinion	Number	Per cent	Number	Per cent
Three hours	13	52.00	2	50.00
Four Hours	8	32.00	1	25.00
No time limit	4	16.00	1	25.00
Total	**25**	**100.00**	**4**	**100.00**

Source : Information collected through questionnaire.

of opinions. Hence, it is suggested that the meeting time may be extended beyond one hour based on the various requirements of the meeting.

Normally, quality circles hold meeting once a week. Both the organizations also decided to hold the meetings once in a week. But some quality circles may not hold meetings regularly owing to various reasons. Table 5.9 indicates the opinions of the members about the regularity in conducting the meetings. It shows that 58.57 per cent of the members of BHEL and 85 per cent of the members of TISCO expressed that meetings are conducted regularly in their quality circles.

Table 5.9 : Members Opinions on the Regularity of the Conducting Meetings

Opinion	BHEL		TISCO	
	Number	Per cent	Number	Per cent
Meetings are regularly conducted	41	58.57	17	85.00
Meetings are not conducted regularly	29	41.53	3	15.00
Total	**70**	**100.00**	**20**	**100.00**

Source : Information collected through questionnaire.

The members were asked about the reasons for the irregularity in conducting meetings. The reasons identified by the members for conducting the meetings irregularly are presented in Table 5.10. They are : no issues to discuss, (28.12) per cent); heavy production schedule (56.25 per cent); indifferent attitude of the circle leader (6.25 per cent); and non-co-operation of the other members (9.38 per cent).

Table 5.10 : Reasons for Irregularity in Conducting the Meetings

Opinion	BHEL Number	BHEL Per cent	TISCO Number	TISCO Per cent
No issues to Discuss	7	24.14	2	66.67
Busy Production schedule	17	58.62	1	33.33
Indifference attitude of circle leader	2	6.90	--	--
Non-Cooperativeness of the other Members	3	10.34	--	--
Total	**29**	**100.00**	**3**	**100.00**

Source **: Information collected through questionnaire.**

Members' Attendance

Members' full attendance at the meetings is necessary to discuss the issues thoroughly and to take important decisions. Presentation of different opinions of the members and meaningful discussions on each issue will be possible only if the attendance is full and regular, such an attendance shapes up effective decisions. The management of both the organizations stated that the average percentage of attendance of the members at the circle meetings is around, 70.[1]

The opinions of members about the regularity in attending the meetings are shown in Table 5.11. It is observed from this table that the majority of the meetings i.e., 47.14 per cent from BHEL and 60.00 per cent from TISCO, are regular in attending the meetings. Members who expressed that they are irregular to the meetings include 20.00 per cent from BHEL and 25.00 per cent from TISCO. As many as 32.86 per cent members from BHEL and 15 per cent members from TISCO opined that they attend the meetings some times only. Comparative analysis shows that the attendance of the members is more in TISCO than in BHEL. The members opinion about the fellow members' attendance will be useful in coming to a conclusion as some members made some keen observation on the attendance of their fellow-members.

1. BHEL, Quality Circle, Quality Assurance Division.

Table 5.11 : Members' Opinion on the Regularity in Attending Meetings

Opinion	BHEL Number	BHEL Per cent	TISCO Number	TISCO Per cent
Regular	33	47.14	12	60.00
Irregular	14	20.00	5	25.00
Attending some times	23	32.86	3	15.00
Total	**70**	**100.00**	**20**	**100.00**

Source : Information collected through questionnaire.

The members' opinion on the co-members' attendance is shown in Table 5.12. Majority of the members i.e., 60 per cent from BHEL and 90 per cent from TISCO stated that their co-members attendance at the meetings is always full. The members also expressed that the attendance of co-members at the meetings is full only sometimes. Only 7.14 per cent from BHEL and 5 per cent form TISCO opined that the co-members attendance at the meetings is always poor. An enquiry into the reasons for the irregular attendance is necessary to offer suggestions for the improvement of attendance.

Table 5.12 : Members' Opinions on the Co-members' Attendance in Meetings

Opinion	BHEL Number	BHEL Per cent	TISCO Number	TISCO Per cent
Always full	42	60.00	18	90.00
Only sometimes full	23	32.86	1	5.00
Always Poor	5	7.14	1	5.00
Total	**70**	**100.00**	**20**	**100.00**

Source : Information collected through questionnaire.

The reasons for irregular attendance are presented in Table 5.13. The table shows that the majority of the members, i.e., 45.71 per cent from BHEL and 50 per cent from TISCO are irregular in attendance due to the busy production schedule. As many as 27.14 per cent members from BHEL and 20 per cent from TISCO expressed that personal problems are responsible for the poor attendance at the meetings. Disbelief in the implementation of decisions is one of the reasons for irregular attendance as expressed by 20 per cent of members from TISCO. Only 7.15 per cent from BHEL stated that loss of overtime is the reason for irregular attendance. It is, therefore, suggested that managements of both the organizations should take steps to improve the attendance by formulating a schedule which does not conflict with production work schedule, by seriously implementing the decisions of the meetings, by satisfying the workers' social and psychological needs, and by creating the awareness extensively among members. Members' awareness influences not only attendance but also effective functioning of QCs.

Table 5.13 : Reasons for Irregular Attendance of Members

Opinion	BHEL		TISCO	
	Number	Per cent	Number	Per cent
Personal Reasons	19	27.14	4	20.00
Loss of over-time	5	7.15	--	--
Loss of Production	32	45.71	10	50.00
No faith in the implementation of Decisions	14	20.00	6	30.00
Total	**70**	**100.00**	**20**	**100.00**

Source : Information collected through questionnaire.

2. Nature and Extent of Participation

The co-operative nature of participation of members in the meetings is essential for effective decision-making. The nature of members' participation in meetings is presented in Table 5.14. A majority of the respondents, i.e., 64.28 per cent from BHEL and 75 per cent from TISCO, expressed that the members' participation in the meetings is co-operative. As many as 15 members (21.43 per cent) from BHEL and three members from TISCO stated that the members' participation in the meetings is reasonably good. The indifferent attitude of some members may effect the quality of decisions.

Members have to express their opinions, discuss the issues and offer solutions freely and frankly and openly. Openness in the discussions facilitates effective decisions. Table 5.15 shows the degree of openness in discussions. Openness in discussions is upto 40 per cent as expressed by 25 members from BHEL, and four members from both the organizations opined that 60 per cent of the discussions has openness. Eighty per cent of the discussions are open as perceived by fifteen per cent members from BHEL and ten per cent from TISCO. A few members from both the organizations stated that cent per cent of the discussions are open.

Table 5.14 : Nature of Members Participation in Meetings

Nature of Participation	BHEL		TISCO	
	Number	Per cent	Number	Per cent
Co-operative	45	64.28	15	75.00
Reasonably good	15	21.43	3	15.00
Indifferent	10	14.29	2	10.00
Total	**70**	**100.00**	**20**	**100.00**

Source : Information collected through questionnaire.

Table 5.15 : Degree of Openness in Discussion

Degree of Openness	BHEL		TISCO	
	Number	Per cent	Number	Per cent
Upto 20%	--	--	--	--
Upto 40%	25	35.71	4	20.00
Upto 60%	32	45.72	13	65.00
Upto 80%	11	15.71	2	10.00
Upto 100%	2	2.86	1	5.00
Total	**70**	**100.00**	**20**	**100.00**

Source : Information collected through questionnaire.

It is further observed from the table that the degree of openness in discussions is more in TISCO than in BHEL as opined by the members. It is also viewed that complete openness does not exist. Hence, it is suggested that the facilitator and leaders should take steps to enhance openness among the members in discussions.

Extent of Participation

The extent of participation of the members in the proceedings of the meetings determines the level of success of the deliberations of the meetings, in addition to the nature of participation and degree of openness in discussions. Table 5.16 shows the extent of participation of the members in the meetings. It is observed from this table that majority of

Table 5.16 : Extent of Member Participation in Meetings

Extent of Participation	BHEL		TISCO	
	Number	Per cent	Number	Per cent
To the full extent in all issues	4	5.71	1	5.00
To the full extent in interested issues	29	41.43	9	45.00
To the reasonbale extent in all issues	11	15.71	2	10.00
To the reasonable extent in interested issues	14	20.00	5	25.00
To a little extent	9	12.86	2	10.00
Not at all	3	4.29	1	5.00
Total	**70**	**100.00**	**20**	**100.00**

Source : Information collected through questionnaire.

the representatives (41.43 per cent from BHEL and 45.00 per cent from TISCO) expressed that they participated to the full extent but only in the issues they were interested in. A considerable number of respondents (20.00 per cent from BHEL and 25.00 per cent from TISCO) informed that they participated to the reasonable extent but in interested issues only. Significant observation from this table is that 5.71 per cent of the respondents from BHEL and 5.00 per cent from TISCO expressed that they participated in all issues to the full extent. Some members participated to a reasonable extent in all issues. There are cases of participation to a little extent and no participation at all. This disturbing situation of self-centerdness on the part of respondents will defeat the very purpose of QCs. Hence, it is suggested that the respondents should change their attitude and be active in participating and involving themselves to the fullest extent in the deliberations of the meetings of QCs.

3. Implementation of Decisions

After analyzing and discussing various problems, the members of the quality circle develop alternative solutions to various problems. They select the best solution and take a decision and submit the same to the management for consideration and implementation. Table 5.17 presents the number of decisions made regarding the problems in BHEL and

Table 5.17 : Number of Decisions Taken and Implemented in BHEL and TISCO

Year	Decisions Taken		Decisions Implemented		Percentage of Decisions Implemented to Decisions taken	
	BHEL	TISCO	BHEL	TISCO	BHEL	TISCO
1980–81	8	--	5	--	62.50	--
1981–82	22	--	17	--	77.27	--
1982–83	45	--	38	--	84.44	--
1983–84	56	--	41	--	73.21	--
1984–85	78	--	62	--	79.49	--
1985–86	154	--	106	--	68.83	--
1986–87	203	9	180	6	88.67	66.67
1987–88	222	26	192	18	86.49	69.23
Total	788	35	641	24	81.34	68.57

Source : Information collected through questionnaire.

TISCO since the inception of the quality circles. It is observed from the table that the number of decisions made in various quality circles in BHEL increased from 8 to 222 during the period 1980-81 to 1987-88. The total number of decisions made during the period amounts to 788. The number of decisions made in TISCO was 9 in 1986-87 and 26 in the year 1987-88.

The suggestions are presented to the management for implementation after they are arrived at the meetings. The management examines the feasibility of the suggestions presented by the quality circle members and finally implement the suggestion.

The number of decisions implemented is presented in Table 5.17. It is observed from this table that the number of decisions implemented in BHEL increased continuously from 5 to 192 during the period 1980-81 to 1987-88. The percentage of decisions implemented to decisions made varied between 62.50 to 88.67 during the period. It is further observed that 81.34 per cent of the total decisions made were implemented during the period in BHEL. In TISCO also the number of the decisions implemented increased continuously form 9 to 26 during the period. 1986-87 to 1987-88. It is further observed that 68.57 per cent of the total decisions made were implemented during the period in TISCO.

Thus, it is observed from the table 5.17 that cent per cent implementation of the decisions is not possible in both the organizations. As far as the total implementation is concerned, TISCO is better than BHEL.

Members persuade the management to implement the accepted decisions at the earliest as the members feel it as a sense of achievement, and they also co-operate with the management in implementation. But management may not be keen in implementing them immediately. Hence, an enquiry is made to find out the time taken to implement the decisions. Table 5.18 presents the opinions of the members on the time taken to implement the decisions. The majority of the members i.e., 23 (32.85 per cent) from BHEL and 10 (50.00 per cent) from TISCO, stated that the management took six months to implement the decisions. As many as 24.29 per cent of the members from BHEL and ten per cent from TISCO stated that the suggestions were implemented within one month. Management took three months time to implement the decisions taken in QC meetings as reported by 20 per cent of the members each from BHEL and TISCO. Only nine members (12.86 per cent) from BHEL and two members (10.00 per cent) from TISCO stated that more than one years' time was taken to implement the decisions.

Table 5.18 : Time Taken to Implement the Decisions

Time Taken	BHEL		TISCO	
	Number	Per cent	Number	Per cent
One week	2	2.86	1	5.00
One Month	17	24.29	2	10.00
Three Months	14	20.00	4	20.00
Six Months	23	32.85	10	50.00
One year	5	7.14	1	5.00
Above one year	9	12.86	2	10.00
Total	**70**	**100.00**	**20**	**100.00**

Source : Information collected through questionnaire.

It may be concluded that the time taken to implement the decisions varies from one week to one year. But majority of the decisions were implemented within six months. However, it is disappointing to note that managements took more than one year to implement the decisions. This type of practice will kill the initiative of the members in quality circle activities. Hence, it is suggested that the managements of both the organizations should take necessary steps to implement the decisions within a month.

Impact of Quality Circles

Abraham Maslow, in his land-mark work on motivational needs of man in organizations, propounded his concept of `hierarchy of needs' starting at the lowest physiological needs for survival in man to his highest creative need for self-actualization. An employee basically looks for the quality of his work life. The significance of quality in his work life stems from his need for `self-actualization' since he spends almost half of his working hours at the work place, and looks for self respect, for an evidence that he counts, that the jobs he does counts, and that others recognize that he is capable of contributions that transcend the narrow confines of his present job.

The impact of quality circles in an organization can be studied through the growth in production, productivity, labour welfare, and industrial relations.

1. Impact of Quality Circles on Production and Productivity

A quality circle is a voluntary group which meets regularly to identify, analyze and resolve work-related problems. The quality circles have brought quality and productivity to the Japanese industry.[1] QC is basically a problem-solving and participative decision-making group which helps the employees to grow and develop in the areas of improvement in the quality of the product.

The group-thinking and decision-making helps the organization to improve the production and productivity. The quality circle members generally identify some problems relating to the production and they discuss them in the meetings. Every member in the quality circle offers advice based on his skill and background for the betterment of the organizations.

Increase in production and productivity is influenced by several factors including the effectiveness of the suggestions offered by quality circles and their implementations. It is highly difficult to measure the impact of QCs on production.

---

1. Srinivasan, A.V., "Japanese Management," Tata McGraw-Hill Publishing Co., New Delhi, 1990, p. 110.

However, an attempt was made to enquire the members about the impact of quality circles on production and productivity. The impact of quality circles on production and productivity can be studied through the increase in output, reduction in cost of production, elimination of wastage, optimum utilization of raw material, optimum utilization of man-machine capacity, improvement in quality of output etc.

Table 5.19 shows the opinions of the members on the impact of quality circles on production and productivity. The impact of quality circles on the reduction in cost of production per unit is high as reported by 48 (68.57 per cent) members from BHEL and 12 (60.00 per cent) from TISCO. On the elimination of wastage the quality circles' impact is high as expressed by 55.71 per cent of members from BHEL and 90 per cent of the members from TISCO. As many as 46 (65.71 per cent) members from BHEL and 16 (80.00 per cent) members from TISCO stated that the impact of quality circles on optimum utilization of raw materials is high.

The impact of quality circle on the optimum utilization of man-machine capacity is high as opined by 42 (60.00 per cent) members from BHEL and 64 (70.00 per cent) members from TISCO. Majority of the members from both the organizations i.e., 71.43 per cent from BHEL and 85.00 per cent from TISCO expressed that impact of QC is high on the improvement of quality of output. Majority of the members (35 or 50 per cent) from BHEL opined that the impact of quality circles on the increase in output is medium whereas 75 per cent members from TISCO stated that impact on increase in output is high. Thus, it can be viewed that the impact of quality circles on production and productivity is high as viewed by majority of the members.

2. Impact of Quality Circles on Labour Welfare

Welfare in industry implies the provision of medical and educational services, congenial work atmosphere etc. The need for providing such services and facilities arises from the social responsibility of industry, a desire for upholding democratic values and concern for employees.[1] According to Committee on Labour Welfare "it is a broad concept, a condition of well being. It speaks of measures which promote the physical, psychological and general well-being of the working population."[2] Labour welfare is an important facet of industrial relations,

1. Monappa, Arun, & Saiyaddin, Mirza, *op.cit.*, p. 217.
2. Government of India, The Report of the Committee on Labour Welfare, New Delhi, 1969, p. 5.

Table 5.19 : Impact of Quality Circles on Production and Productivity

Areas of Increase in Production and Productivity	Degree of Impact Perceived by Respondents							
	BHEL				*TISCO*			
	High	Medium	Low	Total	High	Medium	Low	Total
Reduction in Cost of Production	48(68.57)	17(24.28)	5(7.15)	70(100.00)	12(60.00)	2(10.00)	6(30.00)	20(100.00)
Elimination of Wastage	39(55.71)	24(34.29)	7(10.00)	70(100.00)	18(90.00)	2(10.00)	--	20(100.00)
Optimum Utilization of Raw Materials	46(65.71)	22(31.43)	2(2.86)	70(100.00)	16(80.00)	3(15.00)	1(15.00)	20(100.00)
Optimum Utilization of Man-Machine Capacity	42(60.00)	21(30.00)	7(10.00)	70(100.00)	14(70.00)	3(15.00)	3(15.00)	20(100.00)
Improvement in Quality of Output	50(71.43)	18(25.71)	2(2.86)	70(100.00)	17(85.00)	2(10.00)	1(15.00)	20(100.00)
Increase in Output	25(35.71)	35(50.00)	10(14.29)	70(100.00)	15(75.00)	3(15.00)	2(10.00)	20(100.00)

Source : Information collected through questionnaire

an extra dimension, giving satisfaction to the worker in a way which even a good wage cannot. The concept of labour welfare assumed importance with the advent of industrialization and mechanization. One of the objective of the quality circle is to improve the safety and working conditions in the organization.

Many factors influence the welfare conditions in an organization. They are, Government's statutory requirements, non-statutory obligations, efforts of the unions and deliberations of participative management and quality circles. Hence, an attempt was made to find out the impact of QCs on welfare measures by soliciting the opinions of the respondents. The responses of the respondents have been presented in Table 5.20.

The impact of quality circles on the congenial working conditions is high as reported by majority of the members, i.e., 56 or 80 per cent from BHEL and 18 or 90 per cent from TISCO. As many as 64 (91.43 per cent) members from BHEL and 16 (80.00 per cent) members from TISCO opined that the impact of quality circles on the improvement of the safety is high. On the improvement of health, housing and welfare, the impact of quality circles is high a stated by 74.29 per cent members from BHEL and 85 per cent form TISCO. Thus majority of the respondents felt that the impact of QC is high on welfare, safety, health and housing facilities.

3. Impact of Quality Circles on Industrial Relations

The management has to deal with employees not only as individuals but also as members of organized social groups. Sound industrial relations play a vital role in the establishment and maintenance of industrial democracy based on labour partnership in the sharing of profits as well as other benefits affecting the interests of workers generally. Quality circle is a group process and there is a constant interaction among workers and between the management and workers. They help as a tool for maintaining congenial industrial relations. The sub-areas identified for the measurement of the impact of quality circles on the industrial relations are (i) improvement in general discipline; (ii) improvement in communication between workers and management; and (iii) improvement in cordial and co-operative relations between workers and management. The opinions of the members on the impact of quality circles on sound industrial relations have been elicited and presented in Table 5.21.

In TISCO not a single man day has been lost on account of industrial disputes during the last forty years. The position in BHEL is also more or less the same. Congenial industrial relations are maintained in both the

Table 5.20 : Impact of Qulaity Circles on Labour Welfare

Areas of Labour Welfare	Degree of Impact Perceived by Respondents							
	BHEL				*TISCO*			
	High	Medium	Low	. Total	High	Medium	Low	Total
Improvement in Working Conditions	56(80.00)	10(14.29)	4(5.71)	70(100.00)	18(90.00)	2(10.00)	--	20(100.00)
Improvement in Safety	64(91.43)	4(5.71)	2(2.86)	70(100.00)	16(80.00)	2(10.00)	2(10.00)	20(100.00)
Improvement in health, housing and welfare	52(74.29)	14(20.00)	4(5.71)	70(100.00)	17(85.00)	3(15.00)	--	20(100.00)

Source : Information collected through questionnaire

Table 5.21 : Impact of Qulaity Circles on Industrial Relations

Areas of Sound Industrial Relations	Degree of Impact Perceived by Respondents							
	BHEL				*TISCO*			
	High	Medium	Low	Total	High	Medium	Low	Total
Improvement in general discipline	35(50.00)	18(25.71)	17(24.29)	70(100.00)	13(65.00)	4(20.00)	3(15.00)	20(100.00)
Improvement in Communication between worers and Management	(53(75.71)	12(17.14)	5(7.15)	70(100.00)	16(80.00)	4(20.00)	--	20(100.00)
Improvement in relations between workers and Management	47(67.14)	15(21.43)	8(11.43)	70(100.00)	19(95.00)	1(5.00)	--	20(100.00)

Source : Information collected through questionnaire

organisations.[1] The impact of quality circles on improvement in general discipline is high, accounting to 10 per cent members from BHEL and 65 per cent members from TISCO. On the improvement of communication between management and workers, the impact is high as reported by 53 (75.71 per cent) members, from BHEL and 16 members (80.00 per cent) from TISCO. Improvement of cordial and co-operative relations between workers and management is highly essential for the effective maintenance of the organization. The impact of quality circles on this aspect is very high according to 67.14 per cent of the members from BHEL and 95 per cent of the members from TISCO.

It may be therefore be concluded that the impact of quality circles on the maintenance of industrial relations is high. But the organization-wise analysis shows that the impact is higher in TISCO than in BHEL.

4. Other gains from Quality Circles

Every problem identified, analyzed and resolved by quality circles, be it of quality, productivity, safety, house-keeping, cost reduction or any other theme, would naturally result in gains that can be qualified in financial terms. Apart from such quantifiable benefits, greater emphasis has to be placed on the long term changes that take place in the organizational culture and style of management as a result of the intangible impact of quality circles.[2] Enrichment of the quality of work-life, better communication, attitudinal changes for better and improved team work, better human relations etc., are some of the other benefits of quality circles. In addition, the intangible gains are useful in the long run.

Table 5.22 shows the opinions of the members on the other gains from quality circles in their organizations. The majority of the members i.e., 62 (88.57 per cent) form BHEL and 18 (90.00 per cent) from TISCO has opined that the impact of quality circles on improvement in attitude is high. On the improvement of personal growth the impact of quality circles is high as expressed by 90 per cent members from BHEL and 85 per cent members from TISCO. As many as 61 (87.14 per cent) members from BHEL and 18 (90.00 per cent) from TISCO stated that thanks to quality circles, the working relationship has improved. Inter-personal conflicts have decreased because of quality circles, according to the majority of the members from both the organizations i.e., 53 members from BHEL and 18 members from TISCO. The majority of the members,

1. BHEL, Personnel Manual and Tata Steel, Concept of Working Together.
2. Udpa, S.R., *op.cit.* p. 114.

Table 5.22 : Other Gains from Quality Circles

Areas of other Gains	Degree of Impact Perceived by Respondents							
	BHEL				*TISCO*			
	High	Medium	Low	Total	High	Medium	Low	Total
Improvement in Attitude	62(88.57)	8(11.42)	--	70(100.00)	18(90.00)	2(10.00)	--	20(100.00)
Improvement in Personal Growth	63(90.00)	7(10.00)	--	70(100.00)	17(85.00)	3(25.00)	--	20(100.00)
Improved working relationship	61(87.14)	7(10.00)	2(2.86)	70(100.00)	18(90.00)	2(10.00)	--	20(100.00)
Decrease in inter personal conflicts	5(7.14)	12(17.14)	53(75.72)	70(100.00)	1(5.00)	1(5.00)	18(90.00)	20(100.00)
Faithfulness towards management	57(81.43)	7(10.00)	6(8.57)	70(100.00)	20(100.00)	--	--	20(100.00)
Creation of Team Spirit	54(77.14)	8(11.43)	8(11.43)	70(100.00)	17(85.00)	3(15.00)	--	20(100.00)
Increase in Problem Solving capacity	58(82.26)	8(11.43)	4(5.71)	70(100.00)	16(80.00)	4(20.00)	--	20(100.00)

Source : Information collected through questionnaire

i.e., 81.43 per cent members from BHEL and 85 per cent members from TISCO were of the opinion that the quality circles have developed a sense of loyalty to their managements. Development of Team Spirit is another intangible gain from quality circles as elicited from the majority of the members from both the organizations i.e., 54 (77.14 per cent) from BHEL and 17 (85.00 per cent) form TISCO. 82.86 per cent of the members from BHEL and 80 per cent of the members from TISCO felt that the functioning of the quality circle has augmented the problem solving capacity of the management.

To conclude, the majority of the members are of the opinion that the quality circles have contributed enormously to the development of human relations in the organization. It is further observed from the table that TISCO has derived many more gains from quality circles than the BHEL.

Conclusion

It is clear from the above analysis that the conditions necessary for the successful functioning of QCs *viz.*, members awareness, conducive environment in the meetings, preparation of list of items to be discussed, duration of the meetings, and members attendance are in existence to a greater extent in BHEL and TISCO, though slight deviations between these organizations are observed. However, it is suggested that management and trade unions of both the organizations should take steps to further improve these conditions.

It is further clear that the degree of openness, extent of participation and implementation of decisions were in discussions, more in private sector organization i.e., TISCO than in public sector organization i.e. BHEL. It is therefore viewed both the management and trade unions in BHEL were not much interested in the successful functioning of QCs. Hence, it is suggested that the trade unions and management should be interested in the faithful functioning of QCs.

The impact of QCs on production, productivity, labour welfare and industrial relations is favourable and high. But TISCO has derived more benefits from QCs than that of BHEL. Hence, it is suggested that the management of BHEL should get the support of top management and encourage the members to make QCs effective and useful.

Evaluation and Suggestions

Management of total quality, maintaining higher productivity, achieving high rate of profitability and managing the business through innovative and creative techniques are not just possible without maintaining harmonious industrial relations. It is more so in a country like India which has to industrialize her economy based of Five Year Plans. Further attainment of plan targets is possible with the maximum contribution of human resources to the organizational goals. In fact, maximization contribution of human resource depends on cordial industrial relations. But it is observed that the industrial relations situation in the country is not conducive fro achieving organizational goals and thereby the plan targets. Workers' participation in management is expected to play a crucial role for maintaining sound industrial relations. Further, it also contributes to the attainment of the individual and group goals as well.

Participation is a mental and emotional involvement of a person in a group situation which encourages him to identify himself with group goals and share responsibilities with them. If workers are given opportunities to participate in the management process there could be positive gains to the organizations' effectiveness and morale. The modern thinking on management is based on considering workers not merely as wage earners but also as equal partners in the productive process. Democratic way of life being a goal of most of the societies, every organization should try to achieve industrial democracy.

The concept of workers' participation in management is as old as the institution of owners and workers. Workers' participation in management can be classified into several forms like informative, consultative, associative, administrative and decisive participation.

The schemes of participative management has assumed a variety of forms and structure in different countries. The scheme of joint consultative machinery in the United Kingdom, emerged with the recommendations of the Whitely Committee, is purely consultative and the areas of discussions are confined mostly to health, welfare and safety of the employees. The scheme is not a much success in U.K. as it had no administrative powers.

The development of participative management schemes is not exclusively a post-war phenomenon in the erstwhile West Germany as Works Councils can be traced back to Bismarck, and developed in early nineteenth century and suppressed by the Nazis. Its revival was with the name of co-determination Act 1976 gave workers a nearly equal voice with share holders in controlling the affairs of the companies. Alongwith, labour unions play an effective role in the co-determination. The working of participative management schemes in the erstwhile West Germany presented a successful record.

In Yugoslavia, self-management gives complete control to workers to mange directly all aspects of industries through their representatives. The important bodies under the self-management are Workers' Council, management Board, Director and Peoples' Committee.

Collective Bargaining is much widely used in the United States of America (USA) as the chief means for industrial democracy. In USA most of the workers and trade unions are not interested in formal participation in management.

In India, isolated instances of worker participation can be found even as early as 1920 in the form of informal joint consultation in the cotton textile industry. After the world War I, the Government constituted Works Committees in printing presses and Railways to promote harmonious relations. A permanent Arbitration Board to settle unresolved disputes was set up in the Ahmedabad cotton textile industry during the same period. Joint committees of workers and management were formed from 1922 onwards in Bengal, Madras and other states. The Royal Commission on Labour observed that the results achieved by the joint committee have been disappointing and recommended for formation of Works Committees. In the year 1947, with the enactment of Industrial Disputes Act, the Central Government required on the establishment of Works Committees in major parts, mines, oil fields and other central

Government undertakings. The First Five Year Plan also reiterated the Government's faith in Works Committees. The Second Five Year Plan however, admitted indirectly that the works committees had not been much of a success and recommended for setting up of the joint councils with representatives both from management and workers. Some organizations like TISCO and Indian Aluminium Company constituted joint councils prior to this. The Government of India sent abroad a study group in 1956 to understand problems in detail in respect of workers' participation in management as it is a relatively new idea. The study group recommended the establishment of Joint Management Councils (JMCs). This scheme is a voluntary one.

The Indian Labour Conference appointed a tripartite sub-committee which recommended the introduction of the scheme in such organizations such as have more than 500 workers, a strong trade union, a fair record of industrial relations and readiness of the parties to try out the experiment. The growth of the JMCs from the beginning was slow as observed in a seminar organized by Union Ministry of Labour in 1958. The Third and Fourth Five Year Plan also emphasized the importance of workers' participation in management. The JMCs were successful in the units where the industrial relations were cordial.

The workers' directors scheme was introduced by some public enterprises and 14 public sector commercial banks in 1970. This scheme was not a success because of the low familiarity of the principles and practice of management to workers' directors.

During the Internal Emergency in 1975, the Government of India announced a new scheme of workers' participation in management as a part of 20-Point Economic Programme. The scheme aims at establishing a two-tier machinery i.e., Shop Councils and Joint Councils in all manufacturing and mining establishment employing more than 500 persons in private, co-operative and public sectors. A report of Ministry of Labour for 1977-78 stated that the scheme had helped in improving production and productivity and overall efficiency as well as the industrial relations situation in the industries. In 1977, the Central Government extended this scheme to other units of service and commercial organizations which employed 100 or more workmen. After lifting the emergency the scheme suddenly lost its effectiveness.

The Government in 1977 constituted a 21 member committee headed by Central Labour Ministry to examine the present scheme and recommend a comprehensive scheme of participation. The committee felt that the schemes of voluntary participation were not functioning satisfactorily and hence it recommended for introduction of a scheme by enacting a legislation. The Government in 1983 proposed the voluntary scheme of participation, covering all public sector undertakings except a few. This scheme could not be successful due to voluntarism. The National Front Government at the centre convened a national seminar in 1990 and elicited the views of various parties and introduced a new bill on Participative Management in 1990. The bill is intended to make the scheme statutory. This bill has not yet taken the form of a legislation.

Though the philosophy and practice of workers' participation in management varies slightly from country to country, its basic objective is to involve the workers in the process of decision-making and management with a view to securing their contribution to the development of organization and the individual. But, the schemes of participative management in India suffer form structural defects like requirements of involuntary participation of the workers, absence of support of the top management absence of legal sanction for implementation of decisions taken in the meetings of workers' participation in management. Hence, it is suggested that the Government and management should take necessary steps to modify the structure of the workers' participation in management in such a way that these basic structural defects are rooted out.

The Report of the Ministry of Labour for 1977-78 stated that about 688 units in private sector in various states introduced various schemes of participative management. Among the private sector units Tata Iron and Steel Company Limited is a pioneering one in introducing workers participation in management. Out of the 244 operational public sector units, only 238 have implemented the scheme. It is said that Bharat Heavy Electricals Limited (BHEL) in one of the Public sector undertaking where participative management is successfully implemented.

Quality Circles

The defect of involuntary participation gave birth to a new concept called quality circles. Quality circle is relatively of recent origin, first experimented in Japan. The basic advantage of this technique over workers' participation in management is voluntary association and participation of members in identifying, analyzing the work related problems and for remedial solutions. This scheme is expected to be complimentary to workers' participation in management and contribute more effectively than participative management to the goals of individual workers and the organization.

In 1962, the first quality circle was launched in Japan under the leadership of Prof. Ishikawa. The concept spread all over Japan and became a movement and has more than ten million workers involved in quality circles in 1989-90. Over forty countries in the world were operating quality circles by the end of 1989-90.

In 1980, Mr. Udpa the then General Manager of BHEL Ramachandrapuram unit, during one of his business visits to Japan observed the operation of quality circles and he had discussions with Prof. Shin Miura of Tamagawa University on the subject. After returning to India he held discussions with different sections of the employees in BHEL. Initially two quality circles were started in two different work areas in the year 1980. Spontaneous enthusiasm developed among the employees in other work areas as the news spread about the success of the quality circles. There were 16,569 quality circles in BHEL by the end of 1988-89. TISCO introduced quality circles in 1986. A national body i.e., Quality Circle Forum of India (QCFI) was formed in 1982 to promote the quality circle activity in the country.

The philosophy of quality circles is, inspire for more effective team work, increase employee motivation, creation of problem-solving capability, development of harmonious manager-worker relationships, promote personal leadership development. Thus it is a people building philosophy.

The Present Study

1. Significance of the Study

The public sector in India is created to launch and control large capital intensive industries, industries involving high risk of return and low rate of profitability. Among the public sector enterprises the engineering industry occupies a premier position in respect of investment and employment. Bharat Heavy Electricals Limited (BHEL) plays a significant role among the public sector engineering industry. It is engaged in the production of specialized heavy electrical equipment like power transformers, industrial traction motors etc., and sixth largest profit-making public sector undertaking in the country.

The private sector plays a dominant role in the economic development of the country. Contribution of the private sector to the net domestic product was 75.50 per cent in 1984–85. It provided employment to 93 per cent of the people working in the corporate sector in 1984–85. Certain industries like the Tata Iron and Steel Company Limited (TISCO), The Tata Engineering and Locomotives Company Limited (TELCO) are the critical, strategic and core industries within the private sector. Among the private sector organizations TISCO occupied first place in respect of turnover in 1989–90.

It is observed that the industrial relations position in BHEL and TISCO has been congenial. This might be due to management of human resources on democratic lines. The scheme of participative management might have played a pivotal role in these two organizations in maintaining harmonious industrial relations. Hence, it is felt that a study on workers' participation in management in these two organizations is of great significance.

2. The Industrial Units under Study

Bharat Heavy Electricals Limited (BHEL) was formed in 1964 to achieve self-sufficiency in producing power generating equipment. BHEL ranks among the top 500 big companies in the world. And it is also one among the top 12 power equipment manufacturers in the world. It has 13 manufacturing divisions which are located in various parts of the country including Hyderabad. It has recorded a steady growth over the past years.

BHEL, Hyderabad unit was established under the framework of the Indo-Czeckoslovakian economic agreement in the year 1963. It manufactures oil rigs, gas turbines, thermal turbines, steam turbines, circuit breakers, compressors, pumps etc. The high quality of workmanship of BHEL, Hyderabad unit has earned recognition from international associations such as the American Society of Mechanical Engineers, American Petroleum Institute etc.

It is observed that the capital and employment in BHEL, Hyderabad unit increased significantly during 1982–83 to 1988–89. It is surprising to note that there were no strikes and lockouts during the period, which is a sign of sound industrial relations.

The Tata Iron and Steel Company Limited (TISCO), India's first integrated steel plant was established in Jamshedpur, Bihar in 1912. It is observed that the TISCO occupies the first position among the private sector undertakings and other steel producing units. It is observed that the capital increased by two-fold, employment rose by 50 per cent, sales turnover increased by nearly two times and profit recorded fourfold increase during the period 1982–83 to 1988–89 in TISCO. No strikes and lockouts were observed during the last four decades in TISCO.

3. Objectives, Methodology and Sampling

The present study is designed and carried out with the following objectives :

a) To examine the structure of participative management forums in the units under study;

b) to enquire into the working of participative forums;

c) to evaluate the impact of participative management schemes, on selected variables; and

d) to study the working of Quality Circles and their impact on selected variables.

In order to attain the objectives stated above, information was collected from both primary and the secondary sources. Primary data was collected through a schedule administered among the sample respondent participants with a view to making the study more objective and meaningful. Informal discussions with the management and union leaders were carried out, with a view to soliciting their rich experiences.

In addition to the primary data collected, secondary sources of information were also relied upon, to the extent needed. Secondary data was obtained from the records of the two organizations viz., Annual Reports, Minutes of participative councils, Personnel Manual, in-house journals etc.

Sampling

It is observed that management and worker representatives are equal at each level in both the organizations.

It is decided to select at least one leader/deputy leader and one ordinary member from each category of respondents from each council. This gives a minimum of two respondents of each category and a total of four respondents from each council. The same ratio is maintained in selecting sample at all levels. It is decided to select the sample at the rate of 25.00 per cent of the population (the total number of members at all levels are 248 in BHEL and 742 in TISCO, the total being 990) based on the stratified random sample technique by following the above mentioned criteria. The sample is kept around 25 per cent to the maximum possible extent. The number of management and workers' representatives are nine each at the apex level council in BHEL. A sample of two respondents each of management representatives and workers' representatives is selected. There are 11 members each at the apex council in TISCO. A sample of two each at the management and workers' representatives is selected on the basis of the above mentioned criteria. There are two councils at the plant level and 22 members each of management and workers' representatives in BHEL. A sample of four members of the management and workers' representatives is selected. There is only one joint works council and 13 members each of management and workers' representatives in TISCO. A sample of two representatives each of management and worker is selected.

There are 12 shop councils and 93 members each at the lower level in BHEL. A sample of 24 members each of management and workers' representatives is selected in BHEL. There are 47 shop councils and 347 members each management and workers' representatives at the lower level in TISCO. A sample of 94 members each of management and workers' representatives is selected based on the above mentioned criteria.

There are 352 quality circles functioning in 30 functional areas in BHEL in different departments. Similarly, there are only 12 quality circles in 10 major functional areas in TISCO. A sample of 10 major functional areas in TISCO. A sample of 10 per cent of the total quality circles is selected on the basis of stratified random sampling techniques representing at least one from each major functional areas. Thus, 35 quality circles representing all the major functional areas are selected in BHEL. Ten quality circles one from each of the functional areas are selected from TISCO. The percentage of the sample is more than 10.00 per cent in case of TISCO as there are only 10 circles in ten areas.

Presentation of the Study

The study is presented in Six Chapters.

Chapter–1 outlines industrial relations, participative management schemes and quality circles. Chapter–2 outlines the objectives, methodology, sampling and the industrial units under study.

The structure and working of the participative management are presented in Chapter–3. Whereas Chapter–4 measures the impact of participative management on the organizations' production, working conditions, welfare etc.

Chapter–5 reviews the working and impact of quality circles in the organizations, and Chapter–6 presents evaluation and suggestions.

Structure and Working of Participative Management Schemes

The scheme of participative management was introduced at the apex level in BHEL in the form of National Bi–partite Joint Committee in 1973. It was introduced at the middle and lower level consisting of Joint Councils at middle level and Shop Councils at the grass-root level in 1975. There were the unsuccessful attempts to introduce participative management in TISCO before 1948. However, successful attempts were made by establishing participative management in the name of Joint Consultative Council of Management (JCCM) of the apex level, Joint Works Council (JWC) at middle level and Joint Department Council (JDC) at grass-root level in 1956.

The structure of participative management in BHEL consists of 12 Shop Councils one for each shop/department, two Joint Councils one for each plant and Joint Committee at apex level. Whereas in TISCO there are 47 JDCs at departmental level, one JWC at the middle level and one JCCM at apex level. It is observed that the scheme is not extended to the level of Board of Directors in both the organizations. The scheme in both the organizations is recommendatory. Hence, it is suggested that the managements of both the organizations should convert the schemes of participative management at apex level as the scheme at Board of Directors level as proposed in Workers' Participation in Management Bill, 1990. It is further suggested that the schemes in both the organizations at all levels should be delegated with the authority of decision-making.

Each council in both the organizations is administered by a Chairman, Vice-Chairman and a Secretary. Each council in TISCO constitutes a small agenda sub-committee to prepare the agenda of council meetings. In BHEL, the Secretary of the council prepares the agenda. It is difficult to the Secretary to collect the issues and finalize the agenda, and it may give rise to suspicions to the members. Hence, it is suggested that the BHEL management should constitute an agenda sub-committee.

Objectives and Functions of Participative Management in BHEL and TISCO

The main objectives of the participative management schemes in both the organizations are, to improve production, welfare, satisfy the workers urge for self–expression.

It is observed that the management of both the organizations could not consider the important objectives of participative management like democratization of work place, human growth and dignity of work. Hence, it is suggested that these should also be incorporated in the objectives of participative councils and functions of participative management scheme should also be modified accordingly.

It is observed that workers and management representatives in both the organizations at different levels are nominated by majority unions and managements as the case may be. But management of TISCO is planning to introduce election system for workers' representatives. But majority of the workers as well as management representatives of both the organizations preferred the present system of nomination with a view to avoid political activity in election system. Hence, it is suggested that the management of TISCO should drop the idea of election system in the selection of workers representatives.

The members are nominated to the different councils in both the organizations. But it is observed that there is no clear basis for nomination. The members opined that the members should be nominated on the basis of efficiency in decision-making and in executing decisions. Hence, it is suggested that the bases like hierarchy in designation, seniority in the same cadre should be supplemented by the efficiency in decision-making and executing decisions.

It is observed that the chairman is from among management representatives and the co-chairman from workers' representatives in BHEL and the chairmanship and co-chairmanship are by rotation from among management and workers' representatives in TISCO. But, it is felt that management in BHEL dominate in the proceedings of the meetings. Hence, it is suggested that the management of BHEL should introduce the system of rotation of Chairman and co-Chairman as is the case in TISCO.

Awareness and Interest of Participants

The success of workers' participation in management schemes depends largely upon the awareness and interest of the members about the schemes. But it is observed that the members do not have awareness and are not interested in the participative management schemes in both the organizations. Hence, it is suggested that the managements of both the organizations should educate the representatives about the concepts and advantages of participative management.

The members of the participative management schemes should also know the objectives and functions of the participative management forums in addition to having an idea about the concept of participative management. It is observed that majority of the members from both the organizations have had knowledge of participative management only after becoming the members of the schemes though they are highly interested in the scheme. Hence, it is suggested that the management has to conduct awareness programmes for all the members and non-members about the schemes.

Effective working of the schemes depends upon various factors like active involvement of the members in preparing the agenda. It is observed that the members of BHEL shop council are active compared to those of TISCO in proposing the number of items. On the other hand, the members of TISCO at middle and apex levels are active compared to those of BHEL. It is further observed that members of TISCO are frequently proposing issues than in BHEL. It is learnt that the negative attitude of management and existence of suggestion scheme are responsible to this situation. Hence, it is suggested that the management should offer an in-built incentives in the participative schemes in addition to creating a positive environment and an opportunity to enable the members to propose the issues.

Proposing too many issues frequently may not contribute to the success of the participative management as some of the issues may not be proper for discussion. But, it is observed that the issues which do not fall in the scope of participative management were also discussed. Hence, it is suggested that the management should educate the members regarding the issues to be proposed.

The activeness of the non-members also helps for effective working of the participative management. It is observed that the non-members proposed important issues. It is suggested that the management should further encourage the non-members in order to keep up the same tempo in this aspect.

Normally, all the issues proposed can not be included on the agenda due to various reasons. It is observed that the reasons for non-inclusion of all the items was due to proposing of issues beyond the scope of participative management. Hence, it is suggested that management should educate the members to propose the issues which fall within the scope of participative management.

The agenda should be prepared by mutual consultation in order to streamline the discussions. But it is observed that the agenda was finalized without consultation. Hence, it is suggested that management of both the organizations should caution the officer-in-charge of the committee against such practices.

It is observed that always agenda is not circulated in time to all the members in BHEL. This is mostly due to the indifferent attitude of secretarial staff. Hence, it is suggested that the secretary of the council concerned should be utmost serious in sending the agenda and or notices in time.

Normally, the members after receiving the agenda and notice of the meeting, attend the meeting and discuss the issues. But some of the members sometimes may not attend the meetings owing to various reasons. The percentage of attendance of the members at the meetings shows that TISCO fares slightly better than BHEL in overall attendance. But the absenteeism is around 23 per cent in both the organizations. The reason for absenteeism as perceived by the members are, absence of information about the meeting schedule, absence of faith in implementation of decisions, loss of over time and loss of production targets. Thus the absenteeism is mostly due to the irregularities in the structure and working of participative management schemes. Hence, it is suggested that the structure should be modified in such a way that it does not affect the production target and the overtime allowance of the workers and ensures the implementation of decisions.

Members of various councils are generally supplied with adequate information on each issue of the agenda in the form of explanation or note to the agenda. But it is observed that the workers' representatives at grass-root level felt that adequate information is not supplied to them regularly. At the middle and apex levels the case is better than the grass-root level. Hence, it is suggested that the chairman of the council concerned should ensure supply of adequate information on all the items of the meetings.

Participative management councils take up and discuss various items based on their significance, their necessity and the scope of the council. It is observed that in BHEL, 4,200 items were discussed wherein TISCO 38,524 were discussed upto March, 1988. The main emphasis has been given to production and productivity, and safety in both the organizations. The issues relating to absenteeism were discussed extensively in TISCO, whereas issues on welfare were discussed extensively in BHEL. But it is observed that the important issues like production policy were not discussed at top level councils in both the organizations.

This major lacuna should be checked by the management at the top level. It is further observed that the personnel issues were also discussed in participative management schemes. Hence, it is suggested that the management should take steps to discuss personnel issues mostly in grievance machinery, collective bargaining and other forums rather than in participative management.

A conducive psychological and social environment in addition to physical environment plays a significant role in the successful conduct of the meetings. It is observed that congenial environment was in existence at the meetings. This might have resulted in free flow of communication and active involvement of members. This would naturally contribute to the co-operative nature of participation of the members in the meetings. It is observed that the nature of participation of majority of members was co-operative. But some members' participation was indifferent. The reasons for indifferent participation of the members were lack of interest in the committees, insufficient duration of the meetings, lack of confidence in others etc. Hence, it is suggested that the management should create interest among members through educational programmes and also infuse confidence in others through implementing decisions sincerely. It is further suggested that an element of flexibility in meeting time should also be provided in case of emergency.

The deliberations of the proceedings, the quality of interactions in the meetings and the quality of decisions are mostly influenced by the openness in discussions among members. The analysis of the degree of openness in the discussions shows that the degree of openness in the meetings was only between 41–60 per cent at grass-root level whereas at the middle and apex levels it was between 61–80 per cent in both the organizations. But some members of BHEL expressed that the degree of openness in the discussions was less than 40 per cent. It is suggested that the management of BHEL has to create an awareness among members about the significance of openness through various training programmes.

A less degree of openness generally leads to discussions being dominated by some members or either of the group. It is observed that there were contradictory opinions among the management and workers' representatives at all levels in both the organizations regarding domination. Both the parties accused each other regarding the domination, which shows less degree of openness in the discussions. Hence, it is suggested that both the parties should give up the practice of domination and co-operative in developing free and frank environment during meetings.

There may be a number of hurdles which prevent or hamper the conducive environment in addition to the absence of openness in the participative management. Major hurdle as expressed by the majority of the members was limitations of the management and unions to give out free and frank opinion. Lack of proper understanding, rival attitude, winloose policy might be the reasons for the absence of free and openness of both the parties. Hence, it is suggested that the management should take an active part in discussing the issues openly with trade union leaders and making the trade unions also to be open. Members also experienced an absence of mutual trust and confidence between the representatives. The another reason for ineffective participation was the bureaucratic attitude of the management. Bureaucratic and participative systems cannot go hand in hand. Hence, it is suggested that the managements should restructure their organizations based on democratic principles.

After a thorough and in-depth discussion of each item, the members at each meeting make decisions. It is observed that majority of the members from all levels expressed that they arrived at decisions through consensus. Next highest number of members viewed that they arrived at decisions by voting. There were incidents of accepting the chairman's opinions and accepting the decisions of the group by force. It is, therefore, suggested that the chairman and groups should avoid such type of practices altogether. It is also suggested that, the chairman has to create such an environment for making the decisions by consensus rather than by voting or by any other method.

Though decisions are made by consensus, sometimes, they are thrust on members by the force of the chairman or some groups. Hence, justification of the decisions made may be doubtful. It is observed that the decisions in most cases were made based on merit but some times they were either fully or partially biased. This was due to the influence of the chairman or some groups. Hence, it is suggested that there should not be any force in making decisions. Otherwise, the entire effort of participative management will be a futile exercise.

The secretary of the council prepares the minutes after the meetings are over the gets them approved by the chairman and circulates them regularly to all the members without fail. But it is observed that minutes were supplied to some members now and then and not at all. It is, therefore, suggested that the secretary of the council concerned should be made responsible to send the minutes regularly.

It is always a complaint from the side of the workers that they have to pursue and force the management to implement the decisions. But the management says that they implement the decisions on their own. The opinions of the members shows that, most of the decisions were implemented due to the initiative of workers as stated by both the parties. Hence, it is suggested that management should take the initiative in implementing the decisions. This sustains interest among the workers in the utility of participative management.

The management implements the decisions taken on a priority basis. However, the implementation of decisions in time is more important. It is the ultimate outcome of the entire process of participative management. In BHEL, 43.79 per cent of the decisions were implemented in less than one month whereas in TISCO, 72.35 per cent decisions were implemented is less than one month. But there are several instances of implementing the decisions after three months. This type of practice generally develops an indifferent attitude among the members, and lack of trust in the chairman and the scheme in toto. It is suggested, that the management should not take any chance of using delaying tactics in implementing the decisions. It is unfortunate that a significant number of decisions was turned down. It is also suggested that the management should not think of dropping the decisions.

Impact of Participative Management

Workers' participation in management helps the employees to satisfy the economic, social and psychological needs and to enrich their skills and knowledge. The satisfied and developed human resources are expected to enhance their contributions to the effective achievement of organizational goals. Further, implementation of decisions taken at the participative management helps the organization in achieving its goals. These goals include, maintenance of sound industrial relations, providing better working conditions, taking care of the welfare of the employees, eliminations of sense of alienation of the workers, maximizing productivity and profitability.

Thus, the participative management has its impact on (a) elimination of sense of alienation of the workers, (b) labour welfare and safety (c) industrial relations, and (d) production and its efficiency. It is highly difficult to measure the impact of participative management quantitatively on the various aspects of an organization. Hence, the opinions, attitudes and perceptions of the workers and management representatives are taken up as a basis to analyze the impact of participative management in both the organizations.

1. Impact of Participative Management on Elimination of Sense of Alienation

Alienation may result from poor design of socio-technical systems. Five areas of alienation viz., (*i*) increase in workers' sense of responsibility, (*ii*) reduction of workers' resistance to change, (*iii*) reduction in workers' sense of powerlessness, (*iv*) increase in workers' sense of involvement in work/factory and (*v*) increase in workers' sense of satisfaction are taken up to study the impact of participative management on elimination of sense of alienation.

It is observed that participative management has significantly contributed to the raise of workers' sense of responsibility towards the work. Some members viewed that the participative management did not have any impact because of the absence of required delegation of authority and responsibility to the participants. Hence, it is suggested that the management should delegate required authority and responsibility and make the workers feel a sense of responsibility.

Majority of the members identified that the participative management helped to reduce the resistance to change. But considerable number of members did not visualize any impact of participative management. This may be due to the non-supply of complete information to workers' representatives about implementation of change.

Majority of the members felt that the participative management has reduced the feeling of powerlessness. However, some members stated that there is no impact on reduction of powerlessness and some did not see any clear impact. This may be due to lack of authority or carelessness of management in recognizing the power of workers' representatives. This type of practice hampers the very purpose of the scheme. Hence, it is suggested that the management should make the workers feel about their importance in the organization.

The sense of involvement of workmen in the job significantly depends on participative management. About half of the workers' representatives felt that the scheme did not improve their sense of involvement in work. This might be due to the absence of the sense of belonging. This can be improved by involving them completely in participative management.

2. Impact of Participative Management on Working Conditions and Welfare Facilities

One of the objectives of participative management is to improve the working conditions and welfare facilities. The welfare and working conditions are influenced by several factors like Government's statutory obligations, social obligations, demand of the employees for such facilities in collective bargaining and workers' participation in management meetings etc. Impact of participative management schemes on working conditions and welfare facilities has been studied through the (*i*) improvement in working conditions, (*ii*) improvement in safety, and (*iii*) improvement in health, housing and welfare facilities.

The participative management has contributed significantly to the improvement of working conditions and welfare facilities as perceived by management representatives. It is also observed that about half of the workers' representatives felt that participative management did not improve the working conditions and welfare facilities. This feeling is more in TISCO than in BHEL. The majority of the management representatives from TISCO and the majority of workers representatives from BHEL reported a positive impact. It is, therefore, suggested that the management should be considerate in improving the welfare facilities through the means of workers' participation in management.

3. Impact of Participative Management on Industrial Relations

Four sub-areas *i.e.*, improvement in general discipline, resolution of grievances and disputes, improvement in communication between management and workers and improvement in relations between employer and employee are identified as bases to find out the impact of the scheme. It is observed that more number of management representatives perceived that the impact of participative management on industrial relations is positive. It is further observed that the impact of participative management is high on the industrial relations in both the organizations. But the impact is more in TISCO than in BHEL as viewed by the members. Hence, it is suggested that the management of BHEL should also concentrate on improving employer–employee relations through participative management.

4. Impact of Participative Management on Production and Productivity

The purpose of workers' participation in management in the words of the Second Five Year Plan is to increase productivity in the general benefit of the enterprise, employees and the community. It is observed that the production and labour productivity have been increased significantly in both the organizations. However, it is difficult to conclude that the increase in productivity is due to the impact of participative management.

Seven aspects of production and productivity i.e., output, cost of production, wastage, utilization of raw material, utilization of man-machine capacity, availability of output and absenteeism are identified as bases to find out the impact of participative management on production and productivity.

It is observed that more number of management representatives of both the organizations perceived that the participative management has contributed significantly to the increase in production and productivity. But same is not the case with workers' representatives. This may be due to lack of proper understanding among workers' representatives about the concept and impact of participative management on various aspects of the organization. Hence, it is suggested that the management should undertake educational and training programmes to enrich the human resources of the workers in the areas of participative management.

Quality Circles

1. Origin and Growth of Quality Circles in BHEL and TISCO

The quality circle movement in India was started in BHEL, Hyderabad unit, with five circles, in 1981. They increased to 352 circles with a membership of 3,513 in 1988–89.

The formation of quality circles in TISCO was thanks to their success in their sister concern i.e., TELCO, Jamshedpur, where quality circles had been functioning effectively. The model as well as its framework was based on the TISCO's model. The first batch of 12 quality circles was started in the year 1986.

2. Working of Quality Circles

The effectiveness of the working of quality circles depends on various factors like the length of experience of members in the quality circles, members' awareness and environment in the meetings. Most of the members from BHEL have had three to nine years of association with quality circles, whereas all the members of TISCO have less than three years of experience, as the quality circles in TISCO were started in 1986 only.

Each and every quality circle member should be fully aware of the simple problem–solving techniques. It is observed that majority of the members are aware of the SQC techniques. It is suggested that the management should give proper training on the SQC techniques to the members who are unaware of it.

A congenial environment plays a key role in the successful conduct of meetings. A highly congenial environment is borne out by the majority of the members. The environment is more congenial in TISCO than in BHEL.

It is further observed that the conducive environment at the meetings enabled the members to present the issues frequently. It is also observed that the non–members are also inspired by the conducive environment in proposing issues. The representation from non-members are more frequent in TISCO that in BHEL. However, it is suggested that the management of both the organizations should further involve non-members by creating and continuously maintaining highly conducive environment at the meetings.

The quality circle members in both the organizations meet once a week for an hour. Some times the duration of the meetings may not be sufficient due to various reasons. The opinions of the members on the sufficiency of duration of the meeting time shows that the members are satisfied with the present duration of meeting time. Some members expressed that the present duration of the meeting time is insufficient and they proposed an increase of meeting time to three hours. It is suggested that the meeting time may be extended beyond one hour based on the requirements of the meetings.

Normally, quality circles hold meetings once in a week. Majority of the members from both the organizations stated that the meetings are conducted regularly. But, some members expressed that the meetings were not conducted regularly owing to lack of issues to discuss, heavy production schedule, indifferent attitude of the circle leader and non–co-operation of the other members. Hence, it is suggested that both the parties should plan the schedule properly.

Members' full attendance at the meetings is necessary to discuss the issues thoroughly and to take effective decisions. It is observed that, the attendance is around 70 per cent in both the organizations. The reasons for irregular attendance of some members are busy production schedule, disbelief in the implementation of decisions and loss of overtime. It is suggested that both the organizations should take steps to improve the attendance by formulating a schedule which does not conflict with production work, by seriously implementing the decisions of the meeting, satisfying the workers' social and psychological needs and creating the awareness among members. Members' awareness influences not only attendance but also enables effective functioning of quality circles.

Nature and Extent of Participation

The Co-operative nature of participation of members in the meetings is essential for effective decision-making. It is observed that the members' participation in meetings is co-operative.

Members have to express their opinions, discuss the issues and offer solutions freely, frankly and openly. Openness in the discussions facilities effective decisions. It is observed that the openness in the discussions is more in TISCO than in BHEL as opined by the members. It is also viewed that complete openness did not exist. Hence, it is suggested that the facilitators and leaders should take steps to enhance the openness among the members in discussion. The extent of participation of the members in the proceedings of the meetings also determines the level of success of deliberations at the meeting. It is observed that majority of the members participated to the full extent. But some members stated that, they participated to a reasonable extent and a little extent. This disturbing situation of self-centerdness on the part of some respondents will defeat the very purpose of quality circles. Hence, it is suggested that the respondents should change their attitude and be active in participating and involving themselves to the fullest extent in the deliberations of the meetings of quality circles.

After analyzing and discussing various problems, the members of the quality circles have developed alternative solutions to various problems, select the best solution, take a decision and submit the same to the management for consideration and implementation. It is observed that the number of decisions taken in various quality circles in BHEL increased from 8 to 222 during the period 1980–81 to 1987–88. The total number of decisions made amounts to 788. The number of decisions taken in TISCO increased from 9 in 1986–87 to 26 in 1987–88.

The suggestions are presented to the management after arriving the decisions and the management examines the feasibility of the suggestions and finally implement them. It is observed that the percentage of decisions implemented to the decisions taken is 81.34 in BHEL and 68.57 in TISCO. Hence, it is suggested that the management should take steps to implement almost all the decisions, and encourage the members.

Members persuade the management to implement the accepted decisions at the earliest as the members feel it as a sense of achievement, and they also co-operate with management in implementation. Majority of the members from the organizations stated that the time taken to implement the decisions varies from one week to one year. It is disappointing to note that managements took more than one year to implement some of the decisions. This type of practice will dampen the enthusiasm of the members in quality circle activities. Hence, it is suggested that the managements of both the organizations should take necessary steps to implement the decisions within one month.

Impact of Quality Circles

The impact of quality circles was studied through the increase in production, productivity, labour welfare and industrial relation.

The increase in production and productivity is influenced by several factors including the effectiveness of the suggestions offered by quality circles and their implementations. The impact of quality circles on production and productivity was studied through the increase in output, reduction in cost of production, elimination of wastage, optimum utilization of raw material, optimum utilization of man machine capacity, improvement in quality of output etc. It is observed from the analysis that the impact of quality circles on production and productivity is high as viewed by majority of the members.

Many factors including the functioning of quality circles influence the welfare conditions in an organization. Majority of the respondents felt that the impact of quality circle is high on welfare, safety, health and housing facilities.

Quality circles help as a tool to organization for creating and maintaining congenial industrial relations as it is a group process. The sub–areas identified to study the impact of quality circles on industrial relations are, improvement in general discipline, improvement in communication, improvement in cordial relations between workers and management.

In TISCO not a single man day is lost on account of industrial disputes during the last four decades. The situation in BHEL is almost similar. However, it can't be said that the quality circles alone contributed to such a situation. However, it is viewed that quality circles also played their role in this respect.

Every problem identified, analyzed and resolved by quality circles. Apart from the quantifiable benefits, there would be non-tangible benefits due to working of quality circles. Majority of the members are of the opinion that the quality circles have contributed enormously to the development of human relations in the organization. It is further observed that TISCO has derived many more gains from quality circles than the BHEL.

Conclusion

The contribution of workers' participation in management and quality circles to industrial relations can be further enhanced in both the organizations by modifying the organizational structure in a more democratic way and by practicing the democratic principles to a greater extent in all the stages of participative management forums. Top management's commitment and support to participative management and quality circles particularly in implementing the decisions are a must without which the system may collapse.

Bibliography

Books

Agarwal, R.D., *Dynamics of Labour Relations in India*, Tata McGraw–Hill Publishing Company Ltd., New Delhi, 1974.

Ahuja, K.K., *Organization Growth and Development*, Kalynai Publishers, New Delhi, 1979.

Alexander, K.C., *Participative Management : The Indian Experience*. Shri Ram Centre for Industrial Relations and Human Resources, New Delhi, 1972.

Allen, L.A., *Professional Management,* McGraw–Hill Publishing Co., Kagakusha, Tokyo.

American Management Association, *Management and its People,* D.B. Taraporevala, Bombay, 1965.

Armstrong, M., *Principles and Practice of Personnel Management,* Kogan Page, London, 1977.

Arthur, Ross, M., *The Prospects of Industrial Conflicts, Industrial Relations*, Indian Institute of Personnel Management, Calcutta, 1961.

Aziz, Abdul., Workers' *Participation in Management : Indian Experiences*, Asish Publishing House, New Delhi, 1980.

Banks, J.A., *Industrial Participation*, Liverpool University Press, Liverpool, 1963.

Basu, K.S., *New Dimensions in Personnel Management,* Macmillan Publishing Co., Inc., New York, 1979.

Beach, Dale, S., *Personnel, The Management of People at Work,* Macmillan Publishing Co., Inc., New York, 1975.

Bethel, L.L., Atwater, F.J., Smith, G.H.E., and Stackman, H.A., *Industrial Organization and Management*, McGraw–Hill Book Company, Inc., New York, 1971.

Bhagoliwal, T.N., *Economics of Labour and Industrial Relations*, Sahitya Bhavan, Agra, 1985.

-----------, *Personal Management and Industrial Relations*, Sahitya Bhavan, Agra, 1986.

Bhir, B.S., *Dimensions of Industrial Relations in India*, United Asia Publications, Bombay, 1970.

Brannen, P., Batstone, E., Fatchett, D.J. and White, P., *The Worker Directors : A Sociology of Participation*, Hutchinson, London, 1977.

Casico, W., *Applied Psychology in Personnel Management*, Reston Publishing Company, Inc., Reston, Virginia, 1970.

Chatterjee, N.N., *Management of Personnel in Indian Enterprises*, Allied Book Agency, Calcutta, 1986.

Chaudhuri, M.R., *Iron and Steel Industry of India : An Economic Geographic Appraisal*, Oxford and IBH Publishing Company, Calcutta, 1975.

Chadda, Somesh, *Participative Management in Public Enterprises*, Deep and Deep Publications, New Delhi, 1989.

Clarke, R.O. Fatchett, D.J. and Roberts, B.C., *Workers' Participation in Management in Britain*, Heineman, London, 1972.

Cole, G.D.H., *The Case for Indsutrial Partnership*, Macmillan and Co. Ltd., London, 1957.

Das, Nabagopal, *Experiments in Industrial Democracy*, Asia Publishing House, Bombay, 1964.

Datt, Ruddar and Sundharam, K.P.M., *Indian Economy,* S. Chand & Company (P) Ltd., New Delhi, 1989.

Davar, R.S., *Personnel Management and Industrial Relations in India,* Vikas Publishing House Pvt. Ltd., New Delhi, 1981.

Davis, Keith, *Human Relations in Business*, Tata McGraw–Hill Book Company, New Delhi, 1962.

--------, *Human Behaviour at Work*, Tata McGraw–Hill Publishing Co., Ltd., New Delhi, 1989.

Dayal, S., *Industrial Relations System in India : A Study of Vital Issues,* Sterling Publishers, Pvt. Ltd., New Delhi, 1980.

Dougles, Harries, H. and Frederick, B. Charey, *Human Factor in Quality Assurance,* John Wiley & Sons, New York, 1969.

Drucker, Peter, F., *Management : Task, Responsibilities*, Practices, William Haimann, London, 1973.

Dwivedi, R.S., *Dynamics of Human Behaviour At Work*, Oxford and IBH Publishing Co., New Delhi, 1981.

Employees' Federation of India, *Worker Participation in Management*, EFI, Bombay, 1965.

Flippo, E.B., *Personnel Management,* McGraw–Hill International Book Company, Tokyo, 1981.

French, Wandell, L., *The Personnel Management Process,* Houghton Mifflin Company, Boston, 1978.

Gangadhara Rao, M., and Subba Rao, P., *Human Resources Management in Indian Railways*, Manas Publications, New Delhi, 1986.

Gangadhara Rao, M., Rao, V.S.P. and Narayana, P.S., *Organizational Behaviour, Text and Cases*, Konark Publishers Pvt. Ltd., New Delhi, 1987.

Gangadhara Rao, M., Subba Rao, P. and Rao, V.S.P., *Human Resources Management in Public Sector,* Himalaya Publishing House, Bombay, 1961.

Ganguli, H.C., *Industrial Productivity and Motivation*, Asia Publishing House, Bombay, 1961.

Ghosh, Biswanath, *Personnel Management and Industrial Relations—Its Nature and Practice in India*, The World Press Pvt., Ltd., Calcutta, 1987.

Ghosh, P., and Nath, S., *Labour Relations in India,* Sudha Publications Pvt. Ltd., New Delhi, 1973.

Giri, V.V., *Labour Problems in Indian Industry*, Asia Publishing House, Bombay, 1972.

Guest, D. and Fatchett, D., *Workers' Participation : Individual Control and Performance*, Institute of Personnel Management, London, 1974.

Gupta, K.L., *Industrial Democracy in Public Enterprises in India,* Navman Prakashan, Aligarh, 1979.

Hamey, W.V., *Communication and Organization Behaviour*, Richard D. Irwin, Inc., Homewood, Illinois, 1973.

Hespe, G.W.A. and Little, A., *Some Aspects of Employee Participation,* In Warr P.B. (Ed), Psychology at Work, Harmondsworth, Penguin, 1971.

Howard, M. Wachtel, *Workers Management and Workers' Wages in Yugozlavia : The Theory and Practice of Participatory Socialism,* Cornell University Press, Ithaca and London, 1973.

Huneryager, S.G., Heckmann, J.L., *Human Relations in Management,* D.B. Taraporawala Sons & Co., Pvt. Ltd., Bombay, 1972.

Ichak, A., *Industrial Democracy : Yugoslov Style*, The Free Press, New York, Collier-Macmillan Ltd., London, 1971.

I. L. O., *Participation of Workers in Decisions within Undertakings,* I.L.O. Office, Geneva, 1969.

Johnson, William, A., *The Steel Industry in India,* Oxford University Press, Bombay, 1967.

Jucius Micheal, *Personnel Management*, D.B. Taroporewala & Sons, Bombay, 1984.

Kannappan, Subbaiah, *Workers' Participation in Management : A Review of Indian Experience*, Bulletin of International Institute of Labour Studies, No. 5, November, 1968.

Kast, F.E. and Rosenzweig, J.E., *Organization and Management*, McGraw–Hill Publishing Company, New York, 1984.

Kaulgi, R.G., *The Strategy and Tactics at the Bargaining Table*, in Y.B. Bhonsle (Ed.) *Personnel Management, The Indian Scene*, S. Chand & Co., New Delhi, 1977.

Kennedy, Van, D., *Unions, Employers and Government, Essays on Indian labour Questions*, Manaktala and Sons, Bombay, 1966.

King, W.L.M., *Industry and Humanity*, The MacMillan Co., of Canada Ltd., Toronto, 1935.

Kolaja, J., *Workers' Councils : The Yogoslav Experience*, Tavistock Publications, London, 1965.

Koontz, M., O'Donell, D., Weihrich, H., *Management*, McGraw–Hill, New York, 1979.

Kudcehedkar, L.S., *Aspects of Personnel Management and Industrial Relations*, Tata McGraw–Hill Publishing Co. Ltd., NewDelhi, 1979.

Kumar, H.L., *Labour Management : Forms and Prospects*, Metropolitan Book Co., Pvt., Ltd., New Delhi, 1981.

Laxminarain, *Workers' Participation in Public Enterprises*, Himalaya Publishing House, Bombay, 1986.

Likert, Rensis, *The Human Organization, Its Management and Value*, McGraw–Hill, Tokyo, 1976.

Luthans, F., *Organization Behaviour*, McGraw–Hill Kogakusha Ltd., Tokyo, 1977.

Mamoria, C.B., *Personnel Management*, Himalaya Publishing House, Bombay, 1986.

Mathis, R.L. and Jackson, J.H., *Personnel : Human Resources Management*, Tata McGraw-Hill Publishing House Ltd., New Delhi, 1988.

Myers Charles A. & Kannappan Subbaiah, *Industrial Relations in India*, Asia Publishing House, Bombay, 1970.

Odako, K., *Towards Industrial Democracy : Management and Workers in Modern Japan*, Harvard University Press, Cambridge, Massochusetts, 1975.

Pandey, S.N., *Human Side of Tata Steel*, Tata McGraw-Hill Publishing House, New Delhi, 1989.

Pandit, D.F., *Workers' Participation in Management : The Indian Experiment*, Mimeograph, Report submitted to the Institute of Economic Growth, New Delhi, 1962.

Pant, S.C., *Indian Labour Problems,* Chaitanya Publishing House, Allahabad, 1985.

Pareek, V., Rao, T.V. and Pestonjee, *Behavioural Processess in Organizations,* Oxford and IBH Publishing Co., New Delhi, 1981.

Pateman, C., *Participation and Democratic Theory*, Cambridge University Press, 1970.

Pearse, Arnos, *The Cotton Industry in India*, Manchester, 1930.

Paramanil, S., *Personnel Management and Productivity in Public Sector Industries in India,* unpublished Ph.D. Thesis, Burdwan University, 1975.

Prasad, L., *Personnel Management and Industrial Relations in the Public Sector,* Progressive Corporation Pvt. Ltd., Bombay, 1973.

Pylee, M.V., *Workers' Participation in Management : Myth and Reality,* N.V. Publications, New Delhi, 1975.

Q.C.F.I., *Trainers' Manual.*

Raman, V.A., *Human Relations in Industry : Management by Participation,* S. Chand & Co., New Delhi, 1979.

Ramaswamy, E.A., and Ramaswamy Uma, *Industry and Labour : An Introduction,* Oxford University Press, New Delhi, 1987.

Ramesh, K. and Narasimha Rao, GBVL, *Participative Management,* Ajanta Publications, New Delhi, 1990.

Rao, M.M., *Labour Management Relations and Trade Union Leadership,* Deep and Deep Publications, New Delhi, 1986.

Rao, R.V., *Labour Management Relations : New Perspectives and Prospects,* D.K. Publishing House, New Delhi, 1974.

Rath, B.P. *Workers' Particiaption in Management : An Empirical Study,* unpublished Ph.D., Thesis, Berhampur University, Berhampur, 1985.

Reynold's, Lloyd, G., *Labour Economics and Labour Relations,* Prentice Hall of India, New Delhi, 1978.

Sahoo, K.M., *Industrial Democracy*, Deep & Deep Publications, New Delhi, 1989.

Sahu, Bhabatosh, *Dynamics of Participative Management : Indian Experiences*, Himalaya Publishing House, Bombay, 1970.

Sanjivayya, D., *Labour Problems and Industrial Development in India,* Oxford and IBH Publishing Co., New Delhi, 1970.

Saxena, R.C., *Labour Problems and Social Welfare*, K. Nath & Co., Meerut, 1974.

Seth, A.S., *Role of Collective Bargaining in Industrial Relations in India,* Atma Ram & Sons, Delhi, 1962.

Sheth, N.R., *Joint Management Councils, Problems and Prospects,* Shri Ram Centre for Industrial Relations and Human Resources, New Delhi, 1972.

Singh, B.P. et. al., *Personnel Management and Industrial Relations*. Dhanpet Rai & Sons, New Delhi, 1990.

Singh, H., *Personnel Management and Industrial Relations,* Verma Brothers, New Delhi, 1977.

Sinha, G.P. and Sinha, P.R.N., *Industrial Relations and Labour Legislations*, Oxford and IBH Publishing Co., New Delhi, 1977.

Sivayya, K.V. and Das, V.B.M., *Indian Industrial Economy*, S. Chand & Co., (P) Ltd., New Delhi, 1990.

Srinivasan, A.V., *Japanese Management,* Tata McGraw-Hill Publishing Co., New Delhi, 1990, p. 110.

Sturmthal Adolf, F., *Workers' Participation in Management : A Review of United States Experience,* I.I.L.S. Bulletin, 1969.

Subramanian, K.N., *Labour Management Relations in India*, Asia Publishing House, Bombay, 1967.

Subba Rao, P. and Rao, V.S.P., *Human Resources Management—Text, Cases and Games*, Konark Publishers Pvt. Ltd., Delhi, 1990.

Sud Ingle, Quality Circles Master Guide, *Increasing Productivity with People Power,* Prentice-Hall of India Pvt. Ltd., New Delhi, 1985.

Suri G.K., Bhargava, K., *Problems in Industrial Relations,* Shri Ram Centre for Industrial Relations and Human Resources, New Delhi, 1976.

Tanic, Zivan, *Workers' Participation in Management : Ideal and Reality in India,* Shri Ram Centre for Industrial Relations and Human Resources, New Delhi, 1969.

Tannenbaum, A.S., *Social Psychology of Work Organizations,* Tavistock Publications, London, 1966.

Udpa, S.R., *Quality Circles in India,* Tata McGraw-Hill Publishing Company, New Delhi, 1986.

Varandani, G., *Workers' Participation in Management with Special Reference to India,* Deep & Deep Publications, New Delhi, 1987.

Verma, S.J., Management of Industrial Relations, Vora Prakasan, Ahmedabad, 1979.

Viramani, B.R., *Workers' Participation in Management : Some Experiences and Lessons*, Macmillan Publishing House, Delhi, 1978.

Vishnu Gopal, *Industrial Democracy in India,* Chugh Publications, Allahabad, 1984.

Vollmer, R.J., *Industrial Relations in West Germany*, Embassy of Federal Republic of West Germany, 1973.

Webb, S.J., and Webb, B., *Industrial Democracy 1920*, The Seahm Divisional Labour Party, Germany, 1973.

Yoder, D., *Personnel Management and Industrial Relations*, Prentice-Hall of India Pvt. Ltd., New Delhi, 1986.

Reports and Journals

BHEL, Power to the People through Participation.

— *Personnel Manual*

— *Quality Circle Manual*

— *Quality Circle*

— *Quality Circle at a Glance*

Government of India, *First Five Year Plan*, Planning Commission, New Delhi.

— *Second Five year Plan*, Planning Commission, New Delhi.

— *Third Five Year Plan*, Planning Commission, New Delhi.

— *Fourth Five Year Plan*, Planning Commission, New Delhi.

— *Fifth Five Year Plan*, Planning Commission, New Delhi.

— *Sixth Five Year Plan*, Planning Commission, New Delhi.

— *Seventh Five Year Plan*, Planning Commission, New Delhi.

Tata Steel, *Concept of Working Together*.

— *Constitution of Joint Committees of Joint Consultations.*

— *Corporate Reports.*

— *Human Power.*

Journals

ASCI Journal of Management.

Business India.

Business World.

Capital.

Decision.

Economic Times.

Financial Express.

Harvard Business Review.

Indian Journal of Industrial Relations.

Indian Management.

Industrial Relations.

Indian Labour Journal.

Lok Udyog.

Main Stream.

Manpower Journal.

Productivity.

Personnel Management.

Personnel To–day.

Quality Circle India.

Vikalpa.

Index